# POPULAR MUSIC

# The Popular Music Series

*Popular Music, 1920-1979* is a revised cumulation of and supersedes Volumes 1 through 8 of the *Popular Music* series, of which Volumes 6 through 8 are still available:

| | |
|---|---|
| Volume 1, 2nd ed., 1950-59 | Volume 5, 1920-29 |
| Volume 2, 1940-49 | Volume 6, 1965-69 |
| Volume 3, 1960-64 | Volume 7, 1970-74 |
| Volume 4, 1930-39 | Volume 8, 1975-79 |

*Popular Music, 1900-1919* is a companion volume to the revised cumulation.

This series continues with:

| | |
|---|---|
| Volume 9, 1980-84 | Volume 13, 1988 |
| Volume 10, 1985 | Volume 14, 1989 |
| Volume 11, 1986 | Volume 15, 1990 |
| Volume 12, 1987 | Volume 16, 1991 |

## Other Books by Bruce Pollock

*In Their Own Words: Popular Songwriting, 1955-1974*

*The Face of Rock and Roll: Images of a Generation*

*When Rock Was Young: The Heyday of Top 40*

*When the Music Mattered: Rock in the 1960s*

ISSN 0886-442X

VOLUME 16

1991

# POPULAR MUSIC

An Annotated Guide to American Popular Songs,
Including Introductory Essay, Lyricists and Composers
Index, Important Performances Index, Awards Index,
and List of Publishers

## BRUCE POLLOCK
Editor

 Gale Research Inc. · DETROIT · LONDON

Bruce Pollock, *Editor*
Barbara Beals, *Editorial Assistant*

**Gale Research Inc. Staff**

Lawrence W. Baker, *Senior Editor, Popular Music Series*

Mary Beth Trimper, *Production Director*
Deborah L. Milliken, *External Production Assistant*

Arthur Chartow, *Art Director*
Nicholas Jakubiak, *Keyliner*
Yolanda Y. Latham, *Keyliner*

Dennis LaBeau, *Editorial Data Systems Director*
Theresa Rocklin, *Program Design*
Benita L. Spight, *Data Entry Supervisor*
Colin C. McDonald, *Data Entry Associate*

This book is printed on acid-free paper that meets the minimum requirements of American National
Standard for Information Sciences—Permanence Paper for Printed Library Materials, ANSI Z39.48-1984.

Library of Congress Catalog Card Number 85-653754
ISBN 0-8103-7485-4
ISSN 0886-442X

Published simultaneously in the United Kingdom
by Gale Research International Limited
(An affiliated company of Gale Research Inc.)

# Contents

# About the Book and How to Use It

This volume is the sixteenth of a series whose aim is to set down in permanent and practical form a selective, annotated list of the significant popular songs of our times. Other indexes of popular music have either dealt with special areas, such as jazz or theater and film music, or been concerned chiefly with songs that achieved a degree of popularity as measured by the music-business trade indicators, which vary widely in reliability.

## Annual Publication Schedule

The first nine volumes in the *Popular Music* series covered sixty-five years of song history in increments of five or ten years. Volume 10 initiated a new annual publication schedule, making background information available as soon as possible after a song achieves prominence. Yearly publication also allows deeper coverage—over five hundred songs this year, instead of about three hundred, with additional details about writers' inspiration, uses of songs, album appearances, and more.

## Indexes Provide Additional Access

Three indexes make the valuable information in the song listings even more accessible to users. The Lyricists & Composers Index shows all the songs represented in *Popular Music, 1991*, that are credited to a given individual. The Important Performances Index (introduced in the revised cumulation, *Popular Music, 1920-1979*) tells at a glance what albums, musicals, films, television shows, or other media featured songs are represented in the volume. The "Performer" category—first added to the index as "Vocalist" in the 1986 volume—allows the user to see with what songs an artist has been associated this year. The index is arranged by broad media category, then alphabetically by the show or album title, with the songs listed under each title. Finally, the Awards Index (also introduced in the cumulation) provides a list of the songs nominated for awards by the American Academy of Motion Picture Arts and Sciences (Academy Award) and the American Academy of Recording Arts and Sciences (Grammy Award). Winning songs are indicated by asterisks.

## List of Publishers

The List of Publishers is an alphabetically arranged directory providing addresses—when available—for the publishers of the songs represented in this sixteenth volume of *Popular Music*. Also noted is the organization handling performance rights for the publisher—American Society of Composers, Authors, and Publishers (ASCAP), Broadcast Music, Inc. (BMI), or Society of European Stage Authors and Composers (SESAC).

## Tracking Down Information on Songs

Unfortunately, the basic records kept by the active participants in the music business are often casual, inaccurate, and transitory. There is no single source of comprehensive information about popular songs, and those sources that do exist do not publish complete material about even the musical works with which they are directly concerned. Two of the primary proprietors of basic information about our popular music are the major performing rights societies—ASCAP and BMI. Although each of these organizations has considerable information about the songs of its own writer and publisher members and has also issued indexes of its own songs, their files and published indexes are designed primarily for clearance identification by the commercial users of music. Their publications of annual or periodic lists of their "hits" necessarily include only a small fraction of their songs, and the facts given about these are also limited. Both ASCAP and BMI are, however, invaluable and indispensable sources of data about popular music. It is just that their data and special knowledge are not readily accessible to the researcher.

Another basic source of information about musical compositions and their creators and publishers is the Copyright Office of the Library of Congress. There a computerized file lists each published, unpublished, republished, and renewed copyright of songs registered with the Office since 1979. This is helpful for determining the precise date of the declaration of the original ownership of musical works, but contains no other information. To complicate matters further, some authors, composers, and publishers have been known to employ rather makeshift methods of protecting their works legally, and there are songs listed in *Popular Music* that may not be found in the Library of Congress files.

# About the Book and How to Use It

## Selection Criteria

In preparing this series, the editor was faced with a number of separate problems. The first and most important of these was that of selection. The stated aim of the project—to offer the user as comprehensive and accurate a listing of significant popular songs as possible—has been the guiding criterion. The purpose has never been to offer a judgment on the quality of any songs or to indulge a prejudice for or against any type of popular music. Rather, it is the purpose of *Popular Music* to document those musical works that (1) achieved a substantial degree of popular acceptance, (2) were exposed to the public in especially notable circumstances, or (3) were accepted and given important performances by influential musical and dramatic artists.

Another problem was whether or not to classify the songs as to type. Most works of music are subject to any number of interpretations and, although it is possible to describe a particular performance, it is more difficult to give a musical composition a label applicable not only to its origin but to its subsequent musical history. In fact, the most significant versions of some songs are often quite at variance with their origins. Citations for such songs in *Popular Music* indicate the important facts about not only their origins but also their subsequent lives, rather than assigning an arbitrary and possibly misleading label.

## Research Sources

The principal sources of information for the titles, authors, composers, publishers, and dates of copyright of the songs in this volume were the Copyright Office of the Library of Congress, ASCAP, BMI, and individual writers and publishers. Data about best-selling recordings were obtained principally from three of the leading music business trade journals—*Billboard, Radio & Records*, and *Cash Box*. For the historical notes; information about foreign, folk, public domain, and classical origins; and identification of theatrical, film, and television introducers of songs, the editor relied upon collections of album notes, theater programs, sheet music, newspaper and magazine articles, and other material, both his own and that in the Lincoln Center Library for the Performing Arts in New York City.

## Contents of a Typical Entry

The primary listing for a song includes

- Title and alternate title(s)
- Country of origin (for non-U.S. songs)

# About the Book and How to Use It

- Author(s) and composer(s)
- Current publisher, copyright date
- Annotation on the song's origins or performance history

*Title:* The full title and alternate title or titles are given exactly as they appear on the Library of Congress copyright record or, in some cases, the sheet music. Since even a casual perusal of the book reveals considerable variation in spelling and punctuation, it should be noted that these are the colloquialisms of the music trade. The title of a given song as it appears in this series is, in almost all instances, the one under which it is legally registered.

*Foreign Origin:* If a song is of foreign origin, the primary listing indicates the country of origin after the title. Additional information may be noted, such as the original title, copyright date, writer, publisher in country of origin, or other facts about the adaptation.

*Authorship:* In all cases, the primary listing reports the author or authors and the composer or composers. The reader may find variations in the spelling of a songwriter's name. This results from the fact that some writers used different forms of their names at different times or in connection with different songs. These variants appear in the Lyricists & Composers Index as well. In addition to this kind of variation in the spelling of writers' names, the reader will also notice that in some cases, where the writer is also the performer, the name as a writer may differ from the form of the name used as a performer.

*Publisher:* The current publisher is listed. Since *Popular Music* is designed as a practical reference work rather than an academic study, and since copyrights more than occasionally change hands, the current publisher is given instead of the original holder of the copyright. If a publisher has, for some reason, copyrighted a song more than once, the years of the significant copyright subsequent to the year of the original copyright are also listed after the publisher's name.

*Annotation:* The primary listing mentions significant details about the song's history—the musical, film, or other production in which the song was introduced or featured and, where important, by whom it was introduced, in the case of theater and film songs; any other performers identified with the song; first or best-selling recordings and album inclusions, indicating the performer and the record company; awards; and other relevant data. The name of a performer may be listed differently in connection with different songs, especially over a period of years. The name listed is the form of the name given in connection with a particular performance or record. It should be noted that the designation "best-selling record" does not mean that the record was a "hit." It means simply that the record or records noted as "best-selling" were the best-selling record or records of that particular song, in comparison with the sales of other records of the same song. Dates are provided for important recordings and performances.

# Popular Music in 1991

There could be no better musical illustration of the metaphorical—if not metaphysical—play on words that the '90s will be a repeat of the '60s, only upside down, than the re-emergence in 1991 of a vibrant, angry, and widespread protest movement in popular songs, inspired at every turn in this decade by black artists and groups instead of whites.

In the '60s, to be young and middle class meant to be white and angry; in the '90s, righteous rage is the near-exclusive franchise of disenfranchised blacks, many of whom were protesting in other ways in the '60s, while represented musically on the pop charts by the acquiescence of Motown and the resignation of Soul. (If Jimi Hendrix momentarily put a guitar torch to the music, his flame was soon doused in the general psychedelic excesses of the day and not heeded.) In the '90s, that the protest movement should be reflected in songs by angry blacks is even more threatening to the white status quo, made up in no small part of many of the same prime movers of the '60s protest movement, now entrenched members of a system wishing these black singers, rappers, and bands would disappear— or at least clean up their language, if not their acts.

## The Dominance of Rap

Emanating from the same underground stream where all the important forms of black music—from blues and jazz to R&B to rock and roll—arose before it, rap has led the way into this protest movement and, like do-wop of the early '60s, has succeeded in uniting the races as no political movement ever could. While the true political value of rap—to say nothing of whether a fully musically integrated pop chart has anything to do with racial equality in the world beyond the dance floor—remains inconclusive, rap's politicizing value is self-evident. And while its practitioners have been marked for social ostracism, abject censorship, and diminishing airplay, rap continues to attract new converts, drawn by its exciting rhythmic explorations, daring musical mixes and mismatches, street honesty, and gutter language, resulting in an evolving form where the artificial lines of color can be obliterated—no mean feat in a musical system that, over the past twenty years, has moved toward drawing these lines with a firmer hand than ever.

Aiding the cause of rap in 1991 has been the appearance of several breakthrough feature length films, detailing a comparable streetwise image of what it is to be young, poor, and black in this day and age, abetted in many ways by the angry voice of rap in the soundtrack. By offering a dissonant contrast to the harmonious memories of R&B of yore—while at the same time reaffirming its essential rhythmic roots—rap's very lack of recognizable melody is a means to eliminate by its harshness any vestige of comfort that might block the truth from reaching a sedate audience. Vivid in imagery and rhymes, we had "Growin' Up in the Hood," by Compton's Most Wanted, from *Boyz N the Hood*, "I Wanna Sex You Up," by Color Me Badd, and "New Jack Hustler," by Ice-T from *New Jack City*. One of the leading "Gangsta" rappers, Ice-T brought his ominous persona as well as his rap to *Richochet*. Stevie Wonder was enlisted to write "Gotta Have You" for Spike Lee's *Jungle Fever*, a film specifically about black/white relationships. Black/black relationships, especially as perceived from the female point of view, were represented this year by Queen Latifah in "Latifah's Had It Up to Here," BWP's "Two Minute Brother," and "You Can't Play with My Yo Yo," by Yo Yo, featuring Ice Cube. Crystal Waters dealt with a pressing urban dilemma in "Gypsy Woman (She's Homeless)," while the unfailingly radical Public Enemy produced "Can't Truss It" and "How to Kill a Radio Consultant."

Not all of rap was so strident. In fact, after a decade of popularity, some of rap's more assimilated entities reached heights of commercial visibility, from Hammer's corporate turn ("Too Legit to Quit"), to the sit-com cuteness of the Fresh Prince ("Summertime," by DJ Jazzy Jeff and the Fresh Prince). Michael Jackson made the most blatant and popular plea for racial unity, in his ingenious video and accompanying song, "Black and White." While Jermaine Jackson made his own plea for a more limited Jackson family unity, in "Word to the Badd," other acts, both black and white, mined the interracial territory for the common good, among them Fishbone, the black band that continued its landmark punk/funk and reggae explorations in "Sunless Saturday," and Marky Mark & the Funky Bunch, a New Kids on the Block redux, who had a lot of white kids dancing to "Good Vibrations" and "Wildside"—usurping the turf of the vaunted Vanilla Ice, whose whiteface sludge was expunged from the airwaves this year, save for "Play That Funky Music." But surely the union with the most far-reaching implications was that of thrash rockers Anthrax, with the notorious Public Enemy, on the latter's "Bring the Noise," a collaboration in some ways echoing, in some ways paying back, what the Fat Boys did for Aerosmith in 1984 with "Walk This Way."

## Heavy Metal Popularity Continues

Spurred by this merger, the blatant bombast of heavy metal and thrash spoke for a young, mostly white teenage constituency that identified, as have countless of their predecessors, with black anger, conspicuously led by the mega-selling Guns N' Roses ("Don't Cry," You Could Be Mine"), a band that sent shock waves into the heartland, not only in their songs, but in their self-destructive personas, which evoked rock and roll scourges past, like the Doors and the Rolling Stones. Following in their wake, Metallica, long the epitome of underground white noise, debuted their new album at number one, and sent a grim single, "Enter Sandman," toward the top of the charts. Huddled in their nether nightworld of teenage rage, metal fans leaned toward "Hangar 18," by Megadeth, "Been Caught Stealing," by Jane's Addiction, Motorhead's eloquent "1916," "Moneytalks," by AC/DC, and Queensryche's spacey "Silent Lucidity."

## Issue-Related Songs Span the Music Spectrum

But rage and its liberating release wasn't only the province of teenagers and blacks; 1991 found similar sentiments in all forms of popular music. The virtual paradigms of our familial malaise, the Simpsons, got the eight-ball rolling, with Bart's dysfunctional anthem, "Deep Deep Trouble." REM spoke for a disaffected college and post-grad community in "Losing My Religion." Country superstar Garth Brooks detailed the rampaging plague of wife abuse, in "The Thunder Rolls." Ray Stevens was in a comic, but no less timely, mode in "Working for the Japanese." Elvis Costello was his usual dyspeptic self in "The Other Side of Summer." Both Sam Phillips ("Raised on Promises") and Patty Larkin ("Used to Be") brought a personal disillusionment to the table. By year's end, more protest could be heard, in the curiously detached "Smells Like Teen Spirit," by Nirvana, and the return of the populist U2 ("Mysterious Ways").

Indeed, the only remaining shreds of optimism and patriotism on the popular song front of 1991 were directly concerned with events of the preceding year, centered on the liberation of Eastern Europe—by Germany's Scorpions ("Wind of Change") and England's Jesus Jones ("Right Here Right Now"). In America, the hotly-debated—if not so hotly-contested—Gulf war with Iraq resulted in the emotional acceptance not only of Bette Midler's version of "From a Distance," but also Styx's "Show

Me the Way," "The Eagle," by Waylon Jennings, the Canadian "Voices That Care," as sung by a "We Are the World"-like conglomerate of voices, and Whitney Houston's incomparable (but subsequently revealed as perhaps technically-abetted) Super Bowl rendition of the "Star Spangled Banner," as public shows of support for our troops.

Superimposed upon a deadly era of safe sex and scant disposable income, as the gulf war quickly came to an end (if not a conclusion), escapism in the form of dancing and fantasy prevailed in 1991, the undisputed role model of which was still Madonna, who freely indulged her penchant for living on the extremes of both, in her various musical ("Rescue Me," "Justify My Love") and non-musical (tell-all bios, know-it-all documentary, see-all photo book) projects. Which is not to say that similar ideas did not impel the Divinyls ("I Touch Myself"), Cathy Dennis ("Touch Me [All Night Long]"), Tara Kemp ("Hold You Tight"), Prince ("Cream"), Naughty by Nature ("O.P.P."), Latour ("People Are Still Having Sex"), C&C Music Factory, featuring Freedom Williams ("Gonna Make You Sweat"), Lisa Lisa & Cult Jam ("Let the Beat Hit 'Em"), or the satirical commentary of Right Said Fred ("I'm Too Sexy").

It is more than coincidental that while the disparate worlds of black and white were joined in rap and alternative music—"I've Been Thinking About You," by Londonbeat, "Unbelievable," by EMF, "Sadeness, Pt. 1," by Enigma—on the dance floor and on the top forty, 1991 also saw the rise of music that evoked the early '60s Brill Building heyday of the do-wop and girl group sound of the Civil Rights era, in the harmonious stylizations of Boyz II Men ("Iesha," "It's So Hard to Say Goodbye to Yesterday," "Motownphilly"), P.M. Dawn ("Set Adrift on Memory Bliss"), Color Me Badd ("I Ador Mi Amor"), Paula Abdul ("Blowing Kisses in the Wind," "Rush Rush"), Gloria Estefan ("Coming Out of the Dark"), and the Triplets ("You Don't Have to Go Home Tonight"). Even Rod Stewart, no stranger to the mating dance, picked up on the prevailing retro mood in "The Motown Song."

### Here's Some Country Music—Call Someone Who Cares

In a world entirely separate from the electric dance hall decibels of two continents, country music experienced a year of popularity the likes of which it hadn't seen since the Urban Cowboy held sway a decade back. With the widespread acceptance of performers like Garth Brooks, Clint Black, Randy Travis, and Kathy Mattea, you would expect a concomitant surge in the eternal verities the music has always championed to add a kind of homespun respite to an otherwise bleak year. However, aside from Mike Reid's "Walk on Faith" and the Judds calling it a career as a mother-daughter act, in "Love Can Build a Bridge," all was not quite warm and cozy in the land of country either. With date rape in high and low places in the news all year, Holly Dunn's innocuous paean to a woman's right to change her mind, "Maybe I Mean Yes," tellingly illustrated how the times had caught up to the message, forcing her to remove the record from the marketplace. Travis Tritt was angrier than most country sufferers, in "Here's a Quarter, Call Someone Who Cares." Mary Chapin Carpenter's Grammy-winning performance came in the form of an ode to rejuvenated nightlife, "Down at the Twist and Shout." Garth Brooks got positively rowdy with popster Billy Joel's "Shameless." The Kentucky Headhunters mischievously rocked and mocked "The Ballad of Davy Crockett." But Amy Grant was in some ways even more heretical, taking a sabbatical from her Christian constituency for a jaunt in the real world with "Baby Baby."

### Hybrid Forms of Music Spread

Straddling country, with its admixture of folk/blues/rock/R&B and pop roots, a hybrid form of music I've been calling Middle of the Dirt Road continued to attract adherents with its message of a somewhat tarnished adult worldliness still compelled by a rock and roll yearning for a better place. That mood and that yearning and that place was epitomized in 1991 most notably by Marc Cohn in "Walking in Memphis." But he was far from alone in his sentiments. You had Robbie Robertson's "Go Back to Your Woods," along with his recollections of a "Soapbox Preacher." Rod Stewart revived Robertson's poetic "Broken Arrow" for a run at the top of the charts. James Taylor's collaboration with ex-urban novelist Reynolds Price resulted in "Copperline." Bonnie Raitt was back in Grammy form, in the up-tempo but not excessively peppy "Something to Talk About." Joni Mitchell touched a nostalgic nerve in "Ray's Dad's Cadillac." Jonathan Richman harkened back to "1963." Richard Thompson's harkening went further, in his quintessential motorcycle epic, "1952 Vincent Black Lightning." The wistful but not entirely washed out Middle of the Dirt Road mood was exemplified by Donald Fagen's revival of Steely Dan's "Pretzel Logic," Eric Andersen's discovery of the lost "Time Run Like a Freight Train," the cover of the Grateful Dead's "Truckin'," by Dwight Yoakam, the cover of Elton John's "Don't Let the Sun Go Down on Me," by George Michael and Elton himself, and the spoken return of Patti Smith and Fred Smith in the hypnotic "It Takes Time," from the soundtrack of *Until The End of the World*.

Inspired by Tom Petty's "Learning to Fly," and his mentor Roger McGuinn's "King of the Hill," a younger generation joined these and other crusty eminences in the Middle of the Dirt Road. There was the jangling psychedelia of Loud Sugar ("Instant Karma Coffeehouse," "Change the Weather") and the Meat Puppets ("Sam"), the sultry blues of Chris Whitley ("Living with the Law") and the Black Crowes ("She Talks to Angels"), the aching folk/rock of David Wilcox ("She's Just Dancing") and Richard Thompson ("I Misunderstood"), and the unexpected poignance of punk avatars Pere Ubu ("Oh Catherine"). Nanci Griffith continued her meaningful folk/pop merger with "Late Nite Grande Hotel." Kirsty MacColl had some trenchant observations of contemporary America in "Walking Down Madison." Billy Bragg revealed a previously undiscovered physical side in "Sexuality" and "I Wish You Were Her," while rockabilly renegade Chris Isaak reached a sensual peak in "Wicked Game." More specifically female relationships were dissected by Christine Lavin in "Prisoners of Their Hair" and Phranc in "I'm Not Romantic." Jules Shear finally released his own commentary on the formerly weaker sex in "If She Knew What She Wants," previously a hit for the Bangles. Peter Astor updated Leonard Cohen's mordant evaluation of the same eternal Middle of the Dirt Road topic, in "Take This Longing."

In the more mundane realms of traditional Middle of the Road, where danger and nuance, challenging detours, and penetrating self-exploration have been expunged in favor of pop sensibility generally devoid of all exotic influences, the big ballad always stands a chance of garnering a favorable hearing among those whose tastes were formed, if not ossified, back in the pre-rock heyday of the Broadway musical. Oddly, however, in 1991, even Broadway was more in tune with the prevailing adult mood, showing, with the release of Stephen Sondheim's *Assassins* ("Everybody's Got the Right to Their Dreams," "Gun Song"), Lucy Simon's *The Secret Garden* ("Come to My Garden," "Lily's Eyes"), and especially the hip *Song of Singapore*, the potential to one day become as natural a repository for songwriters concerned with the greying of the Woodstock Generation, as the albums of Bonnie Raitt, Joni Mitchell, Paul Simon, Leonard Cohen, and James Taylor, among others.

### The Woeful State of Ballads

The same could not be said of the enduring timeless oblivion of the year's most successful ballads. Michael Bolton established himself as one of the more bankable voices of this emotionally bankrupt genre ("Time, Love and Tenderness"), alongside Mariah Carey ("Emotion"), with this year's Taylor Dayne, Celine Dion, coming up sharply on her right flank ("Where Does My Heart Beat Now"). Proving that the top of the singles chart is still available for a rock band, as long as they don't play rock, Extreme, a capable, second generation Boston bar band in the mode of Aerosmith, forged into national prominence with the slightly schizoid ballad, "More Than Words." Worse than that was the sentimental hoax—albeit a Grammy-award winning one—played on the tear ducts of the populace by Natalie Cole, in "Unforgettable," her magic-of-technology duet with her late father, Nat "King" Cole. But the biggest perpetrator of the ballad's bogus art this year was undoubtedly Bryan Adams, whose enormously popular "(Everything I Do) I Do It for You," benefitting from a most fortuitous placement at the tag end of the high profile epic *Robin Hood*, not only had nothing to do with anything of significance in either subject matter, form, feeling or presentation, but had even less to do with the film to which it was appended—like a smile button on the lapel of a sniveling geek. As such, it was a perfect chilling reminder of insidious songmaking at its best.

*Bruce Pollock*
*Editor*

# POPULAR
# MUSIC

# A

**Addams Groove**
Words and music by Hammer, Felton Pilate, and Vic Mizzy.
Bust It Publishing, 1991/Orion Music Publising, 1991.
Best-selling record by Hammer on *Too Legit to Quit* (Capitol, 91) and
in the movie *The Addams Family*. Veteran tunesmith Mizzy is the
composer of the original theme for the TV show.

**Addictive Love**
Words and music by Keith Thomas, Bebe Winans, and Cece Winans.
Sony Tunes, 1991/Yellow Elephant/Benny's Music, 1991/EMI-
Blackwood Music Inc., 1991/Pookie's Music, 1991.
Best-selling record by Bebe and Cece Winans from *Different Lifestyles*
(Capitol, 91).

**After the Dance**
Words and music by Leon Ware, Marvin Gaye, and Arthur Ross.
Jobete Music Co., Inc., 1976.
Revived by Fourplay featuring El DeBarge from *Fourplay* (Warner
Bros., 91). Was a hit for Marvin Gaye in 1976.

**After the Rain**
Words and music by Matt Nelson, Gunnar Nelson, Mark Tanner,
and Rick Wilson.
Matt-Black, 1990/Gunster/EMI April Canada/Otherwise
Publishing/BMG Music/Second Hand Songs.
Best-selling record by Nelson from *After the Rain* (DGC, 90).

**All 4 Love**
Words and music by Color Me Badd, words and music by Howie
Thompson.
Me Good, 1991/Howie Tee/Irving Music Inc.
Best-selling record by Color Me Badd from *C.M.B.* (Giant, 91).

**All the Man That I Need**
Words by Dean Pitchford, music by Martin Gore.
Warner-Tamerlane Publishing Corp., 1990/Body Electric
   Music/Fifth to March.
Best-selling record by Whitney Houston from *I'm Your Baby Tonight*
   (Arista, 90).

**All the Way Home**
Words and music by Bruce Springsteen.
Bruce Springsteen Publishing, 1991.
Introduced by Southside Johnny & The Asbury Jukes on *Better Days*
   (Impact, 91).

**All This Time**
Words and music by Sting.
Magnetic, England, 1991/Blue Turtle.
Best-selling record by Sting from *The Soul Cages* (A & M, 91).

**American Music**
Words and music by Gordon Gano.
Gorno Music, 1991.
Introduced by Violent Femmes on *Why Do Birds Sing* (Slash, 91).

**And Hiding Away**
Words and music by Karen Peris, music by Donald Peris.
Island Music, 1991/Umbrella Day Music.
Introduced by Innocence Mission on *Umbrella* (A & M, 91).

**And the World Goes Round**
Words by Fred Ebb, music by John Kander.
Fiddleback Music Publishing Co., Inc., 1990.
Introduced by Brenda Pressley in the revue *And the World Goes
   Round*.

**Angel**
Words and music by Patrick Moten, Sandra Sully, and Anita Baker.
Moriel, 1983/Spaced Hands Music/Beverly Glen Publishing.
Best-selling record Anita Baker from *The Songstress* (Elektra, 83, 91).

**Angel Dressed in Black**
Words and music by Warren Zevon.
Zevon Music Inc., 1991/Warner-Tamerlane Publishing Corp.
Introduced by Warren Zevon on *Mr. Bad Example* (Giant/Reprise).

**Angels**
Words and music by Peter Holsapple and Chris Stamey.
Pertaining To Music, 1990/Shangmoto Songs, 1990.
Introduced by Holsapple and Stamey on *Mavericks* (RNA, 90).

**Anymore**
Words and music by Travis Tritt and Jill Colucci.
Sony Tree, 1991/Post Oak/EMI-April Music Inc./Heartland Express.
Best-selling record by Travis Tritt from *It's All About to Change* (Warner Bros., 91).

**Are You Lonely for Me**
Words and music by Edwin Nicholas, Mike Ferguson, and Joe Little.
Trycep Publishing Co., 1991/Ramal Music Co./Rude News/Mike Ferguson Music Co.
Best-selling record by Rude Boys from *Rude Awakenings* (Atlantic, 90).

**Are You Lovin' Me Like I'm Lovin' You**
Words and music by Johnny Cunningham and Steve Stone.
WB Music Corp., 1991/Warner-Tamerlane Publishing Corp./Foon Tunes/Sunstorm.
Best-selling record by Ronnie Milsap from *Back to the Grindstone* (RCA, 91).

**Around the Way Girl**
Words and music by Marlon Williams, James Todd Smith, and Rick James.
E.M. Marl, 1991/L.L. Cool J Music/Def Jam/Stone City Music/National League Music.
Best-selling record by L.L. Cool J from *Mama Said Knock You Out* (Def Jam, 90).

**Arrest the President**
Words and music by Percy Lee Chapman and Marlon Williams.
E.M. Marl.
Introduced by Intelligent Hoodlum (A & M, 91).

# B

**Baby Baby**
Words and music by Amy Grant and Keith Thomas.
Age to Age, 1991/Edward Grant/Yellow Elephant/Reunion.
Best-selling record by Amy Grant from *Heart in Motion* (A & M, 91).
  Nominated for Grammy Awards, Record of the Year and Song of
  the Year.


**Baby I'm Ready**
Words and music by Gerald Levert and Marc Gordon.
Trycep Publishing Co., 1990/Willesden Music, Inc.
Best-selling record by Levert from *Rope a Dope Style* (Atlantic, 90).

**Backlash**
Words and music by Joan Jett and Paul Westerberg.
Lagunatic Music, 1991/NAH Music.
Introduced by Joan Jett on *Notorious* (Blackheart/Epic Associated,
  91).

**The Ballad of Davy Crockett**
Words and music by Tom Blackburn and George Bruns.
Wonderland Music Co., Inc., 1955.
Revived by The Kentucky Headhunters on *Electric Barnyard*
  (Polygram, 91).

**Ballad of Gunther Johnson**
Words and music by Tommy Malone.
Almo Music Corp., 1991/Luck Skillet Music.
Introduced by The Subdues on *Lucky* (East/West, 91).

**Be My Guest**
Music by Alan Menken, words by Howard Ashman.

Walt Disney Music Co., 1991/Wonderland Music Co., Inc.
Introduced in the movie and on the soundtrack album *Beauty & the Beast*. Nominated for an Academy Award, Best Original Song.

**Beauty & the Beast**
Music by Alan Menken, words by Howard Ashman.
Walt Disney Music Co., 1991/Wonderland Music Co., Inc.
Two versions introduced by Angela Lansbury and by Celine Dion and Peabo Bryson in the movie and on the soundtrack *Beauty & The Beast* (Epic, 91). Won Academy Award, Best Original Song for a Movie.

**Because I Love You (The Postman Song)**
Words and music by W. Allen Brooks.
Saja Music Co., 1990/Mya-T.
Best-selling record by Stevie B from *Love & Emotion* (LMR, 90).

**Been Caught Stealing**
Words and music by Jane's Addiction.
I'll Hit You Back, 1991/Bubbly Orange Stuff/Embryotic/Swizzle Stick.
Introduced by Jane's Addiction on *Ritual de lo Habitual* (Warner Bros., 91). Nominated for a Grammy Award, Best Rock Song of the Year.

**Being Boring** (English)
Words and music by Chris Lowe and Neil Tennant.
Cage Music Ltd., England, 1990/10 Music Ltd., England.
Introduced by Pet Shop Boys on *Behaviour* (ETTI, 90).

**Belle**
Music by Alan Menken, words by Howard Ashman.
Walt Disney Music Co., 1991/Wonderland Music Co., Inc.
Introduced in the movie *Beauty & the Beast* by Paige O'Hara; also on the soundtrack. Nominated for an Academy Award, Best Original Song.

**Bertha**
Words by Robert Hunter, music by Jerry Garcia.
Ice Nine Publishing Co., Inc., 1970.
Revived by Los Lobos on *Deadicated* (Arista, 91).

**A Better Love** (English)
Words and music by Henshall, Jimmy Helms, George Chandler,
    Jimmy Chambers, and Ian Green.
Warner-Chappell Music, 1991.
Best-selling record by Londonbeat from *In the Blood* (Radioactive, 91).

**Big Shot in the Dark**
Words and music by Pat MacDonald.
Mambadaddi, 1990/I.R.S.
Introduced by Timbuk 3 on *Big Shot in the Dark* (IRS, 91).

**Big Town**
Words and music by Ashley Cleveland.
Warner-Tamerlane Publishing Corp., 1991.
Introduced by Ashley Cleveland on *Big Town* (Atlantic, 91).

**Black or White**
Words and music by Michael Jackson and Bill Bottrell.
Mijac Music, 1991/Warner-Tamerlane Publishing Corp./Ignorant.
Introduced by Michael Jackson from *Dangerous* (Epic, 91).

**Blind Dating Fun**
Words and music by Christine Lavin.
Flip-a-Jig, 1991.
Introduced by Christine Lavin on *Compass* (Philo, 91).

**Blowing Kisses in the Wind**
Words and music by Peter Lord.
EMI-April Music Inc., 1991/Leo Sun.
Best-selling record by Paula Abdul from *Spellbound* (Captive/Virgin,
    91).

**Blues for Michael**
Words and music by Joe McDonald.
McDonald Music Co., 1990.
Introduced by Country Joe McDonald on *Superstitious Blues*
    (Rykodisc, 91).

**Book of Love**
Words and music by Warren Davis, George Malone, and Charles
    Patrick, words by Doug Lazy.
Arc Music Corp., 1957/Windswept Pacific/Longitude Music.
Single revived by Ben E. King and Bo Diddley, featuring Doug Lazy
    (Atlantic).

**A Brand New Book** (English)
Words and music by Graham Parker.

7

Geep Music Ltd., England, 1990.
Introduced by Graham Parker on *Struck by Lightning* (RCA, 91).

**Brand New Men**
Words and music by Don Cook, Ronnie Dunn, and Kix Brooks.
Sony Tree, 1991/Sony Cross Keys Publishing Co. Inc.
Best-selling record by Brooks & Dunn from *Brooks & Dunn* (Arista, 91).

**Bring the Noise**
Words and music by Carlton Ridenhour, Hank Shocklee, and Eric Sadler, words and music by Anthrax.
Def American Songs, 1987/NFP/Zomba Enterprises, Inc.
Revived by Anthrax and Public Enemy in *Attack of the Killer B's* (Island/Megaforce, 91). Originally in the film and soundtrack *Less than Zero* (87).

**Broken Arrow**
Words and music by Robbie Robertson.
Medicine Hat Music, 1987/EMI-April Music Inc.
Revived by Rod Stewart on *Vagabond Heart* (Warner Bros., 91).

**Brother Jukebox**
Words and music by Paul Craft.
Screen Gems-EMI Music Inc., 1990/Black Sheep Music Inc.
Best-selling record by Mark Chestnutt from *Too Cold at Home* (MCA, 90).

**Brotherly Love**
Words and music by Jimmy Stewart and Tim Nichols.
Peer Talbot, 1989/Milsap/Careers Music Inc.
Best-selling record by Keith Whitley and Earl Thomas Conley on *Kentucky Bluebird* (RCA, 91).

**Bulletproof Heart** (Scottish)
Words and music by Jimmie O'Neill.
Copyright Control, 1991.
Introduced by The Silencers on *Dance to the Holy Man* (RCA, 91).

# D

**Daddy's Come Around**
Words and music by Paul Overstreet and Don Schlitz.
Scarlet Moon Music, 1991/Don Schlitz Music/Almo Music Corp.
Best-selling record by Paul Overstreet from *Heroes* (RCA, 91)

**Destiny Street**
Words and music by Richard Hell.
Automatic Street, 1982.
Revived by Richard Hell & The Voidoids on *Groups of Wrath* (TVT, 91). Punk rock classic originally appeared on *Destiny Street* (Red Star, 82).

**Disappear** (Australian)
Words and music by Jon Farriss and Mick Hutchence.
Tol Muziek, 1990/MCA Music.
Best-selling record by INXS from *X* (Atlantic, 90).

**DJ Culture** (English)
Words and music by Neil Tennant and Chris Lowe.
Cage Music Ltd., England, 1990/10 Music Ltd., England.
Introduced by Pet Shop Boys on *Discography: The Complete Singles Collection* (EMI, 91).

**Do Anything**
Words and music by Frederick Thomas, Elliot Erickson, and Ingrid Chaver.
Tuareg Music, 1991/Peasantmart/Skyfish Music.
Best-selling record by Natural Selection from *Natural Selection* (East/West, 91).

**Do Me Right**
Words and music by Teddy Riley, David Way, and Heavy D (pseudonym for Dwight Myers).

Donril Music, 1990/Zomba Enterprises, Inc./Ten Ways To
 Sundown/EMI-April Music Inc./Across 110th Street/E-Z Duz It.
Best-selling record by Guy from *The Future* (Uptown, 90).

### Do What I Gotta Do
Words and music by James Harris, III and Terry Lewis.
Flyte Tyme Tunes, 1990.
Best-selling record by Ralph Tresvant from *Ralph Tresvant* (MCA, 90).

### Don't Cry
Words and music by Izzy Stradlin and Axl Rose.
Guns N' Roses Music, 1991.
Best-selling record by Guns N' Roses from *Use Your Illusion II*
 (Geffen, 91). Same song, with different lyrics, was released on *Use
 Your Illusion I* (Geffen, 91).

### Don't Go
Words and music by Thom McElroy and Denzil Foster.
Two Tuff-Enuff Publishing, 1990/Irving Music Inc.
Best-selling record by En Vogue from *Born to Sing* (Atlantic, 90).

### Don't Go Home with Your Hard On
Words and music by Leonard Cohen and Phil Spector.
Stranger Music Inc., 1977/Back to Mono Music Inc.
Revived by David McComb & Adam Peters on *I'm Your Fan: The
 Songs of Leonard Cohen* (Atlantic, 91).

### Don't Let Me Down
Words and music by Eddie Levert, Walter Williams, Terry Stubbs,
 and Dwain Mitchell.
WE, 1990/Dwaine Duane.
Best-selling record by O'Jays from *Emotionally Yours* (EMI, 90).

### Don't Let the Sun Go Down on Me (English)
Words by Bernie Taupin, music by Elton John.
Big Pig Music, Ltd., London, England, 1974.
Best-selling record by George Michael and Elton John from a live
 single (Polydor, 91). Also performed by Oleta Adams on *Two
 Rooms: Celebrating the Songs of Elton John and Bernie Taupin*
 (Polydor, 91).

### Don't Make Me Dream About You
Words and music by Chris Isaak.
Chris Isaak Music Publishing, 1989.
Released by Chris Isaak from *Heart-Shaped World* (Reprise, 89).

**Don't Need Rules**
Words and music by Stephen Shareaux, music by Rob Grad, Mike Marquis, Dana Strum, and Scott Donnell.
Duke T, 1991/Dinger & Ollie/No Rules/Oobe/Dancing Teen.
Introduced by Kik Tracee on *No Rules* (RCA, 91).

**Don't Rock the Jukebox**
Words and music by Alan Jackson, Roger Murrah, and Keith Stegall.
Mattie Ruth, 1991/Seventh Son Music Inc./Tom Collins Music Corp./Murrah.
Best-selling record by Alan Jackson from *Don't Rock the Jukebox* (Arista, 91). Nominated for a Grammy Award, Best Country Song of the Year .

**Don't Treat Me Bad**
Words and music by Bill Leverty, C. J. Snare, Cosby Ellis, and Michael Foster.
Sony Tunes, 1991/Wocka Wocka/Cosby & Ellis.
Best-selling record by Firehouse from *Firehouse* (Epic, 91).

**Don't Wanna Change the World**
Words and music by Jonathan Rosen, Karen Manna, and David Darlington.
Number 9 Music, 1991/Bass Hit.
Best-selling record by Phyllis Hyman from *Prime of My Life* (PIR, 91).

**Don't Want to be a Fool**
Words and music by Luther Vandross and Marcus Miller.
EMI-April Music Inc., 1991/Uncle Ronnie's Music Co., Inc./Thriller Miller Music/MCA Music.
Best-selling record by Luther Vandross from *Power of Love* (Epic, 91).

**Down at the Twist and Shout**
Words and music by John Jennings and Mary Chapin Carpenter.
EMI-April Music Inc., 1990/Getarealjob Music.
Best-selling record by Mary Chapin Carpenter from *Shooting Straight in the Dark* (Columbia, 90). Breakthrough year for the folk/pop crossover artist. Nominated for a Grammy Award, Best Country Song of the Year .

**Down Home**
Words and music by Josh Leo and Rick Bowles.
Maypop Music, 1990/Warner-Elektra-Asylum Music Inc./Mopage.
Best-selling record by Alabama from *Pass It on Down* (RCA, 90).

**Down in the Hole**
Words and music by James Taylor.
Country Road Music Inc., 1991.
Introduced by James Taylor on *New Moon Shine* (Columbia, 91).

**Down to My Last Teardrop**
Words and music by Paul Davis.
Paul & Jonathan Songs, 1991.
Best-selling record by Tanya Tucker from *What Do I Do with Me* (Capitol, 91).

**The Dream Is Still Alive**
Words and music by Wilson Phillips, words and music by Glen Ballard.
EMI-Blackwood Music Inc., 1990/Wilphill/Braintree Music.
Best-selling record by Wilson Phillips from *Wilson Phillips* (SBK, 90).

**Dream to Dream**
Words by Will Jennings, music by James Horner.
MCA Music, 1991.
Introduced by Linda Ronstadt in the film and on the soundtrack album *Feivel Goes West* (MCA, 91).

**Drift Off to Dream**
Words and music by Travis Tritt and Stewart Harris.
Sony Tree, 1989/Post Oak/Sony Songs/Edisto Sound International.
Best-selling record by Travis Tritt from *Country Club* (Warner Bros., 90).

# E

**The Eagle**
Words and music by Hank Cochran, Red Lane, and Mack Vichery.
Tree Publishing Co., Inc., 1984.
Revived by Waylon Jennings (Epic, 91). Favorite tune of American
    pilots during war with Iraq.

**Eagle When She Flies**
Words and music by Dolly Parton.
Velvet Apple Music, 1991.
Introduced by Dolly Parton on *Eagle When She Flies* (Columbia, 91).
    Nominated for a Grammy Award, Best Country Song of the Year.

**Emotionally Yours**
Words and music by Bob Dylan.
Special Rider Music, 1980.
Revived by The O'Jays on *Emotionally Yours* (EMI, 90).

**Emotions**
Words and music by Mariah Carey, Rob Clivilles, and David Cole.
Mariah Songs, 1991/Sony Songs/Cole-Clivilles/Virgin Music, Inc.
Best-selling record by Mariah Carey from *Emotions* (Columbia, 91).

**Enter Sandman**
Words and music by James Hetfield, Lars Ulrich, and Kirk Hammett.
Creeping Death Music, 1991.
Best-selling record by Metallica from *Metallica* (Elektra, 91).
    Nominated for a Grammy Award, Best Rock Song of the Year.

### Every Heartbeat
Words and music by Amy Grant, Wayne Kirkpatrick, and Charlie Peacock.
Age to Age, 1991/Reunion/Emily Boothe/Andi Beat Goes On/Sparrow: The Sparrow Corp.
Best-selling record by Amy Grant from *Heart in Motion* (A & M, 91).

### Every Road Leads Back to You
Words and music by Diane Warren.
Realsongs, 1991/TCF.
Introduced by Bette Midler in the film and on the soundtrack *For the Boys* (Atlantic, 91).

### Everybody's Got the Right (to Their Dreams)
Words and music by Stephen Sondheim.
Rilting Music Inc., 1990/Revelation Music Publishing Corp.
Introduced in the musical *Assassins* and recorded on original cast album (RCA, 91).

### Exclusivity
Words and music by L. A. Reid (pseudonym for Antonio Reid), Babyface (pseudonym for Kenny Edmunds), and Damian Dane.
Kear Music, 1991/Sony Epic/Solar/Macadamian.
Best-selling record by Damian Dane from *Damian Dane* (Laface, 91).

# F

**Fading Like a Flower (Every Time You Leave)** (Swedish)
Words and music by Per Gessle.
Jimmie Fun, Sweden/EMI-Blackwood Music Inc., 1991.
Best-selling record by Roxette from *Joyride* (EMI, 91).

**Fallin' Out of Love**
Words and music by John Ims.
Paul Craft, 1990.
Best-selling record by Reba McEntire from *Rumor Has It* (MCA, 90).

**A Family Tie**
Words and music by Hugh Prestwood.
Careers Music Inc., 1990.
Introduced by Maura O'Connell in *A Real Life Story* (Warner Bros., 91).

**Feels Like Another One**
Words and music by Michael Stokes, Sharon Barnes, Patti Labelle, and James Ellison.
Willow Girl, 1991/Zuri/Budsky.
Best-selling record by Patti Labelle from *Burnin'* (MCA, 91).

**Finally**
Words and music by Ce Ce Peniston, Felipe Delgado, and E. Linnear.
Wax Museum, 1991/Main Lot.
Best-selling record by Ce Ce Peniston from *Finally* (A & M).

**Finishing Touches**
Words and music by Warren Zevon.
Zevon Music Inc., 1991/Warner-Tamerlane Publishing Corp.
Introduced by Warren Zevon on *Mr. Bad Example* (Giant, 91).

**The First Time**
Words and music by Bernard Jackson and Brian Simpson.

Colgems-EMI Music Inc., 1990/Stansbury Music.
Best-selling record by Surface from *3 Deep* (Columbia, 90).

**The Fly** (Irish)
Words and music by U2.
U2, 1991/Chappell & Co., Inc.
Best-selling record by U2 from *Achtung Baby* (Island, 91).

**Flyin' the Flannel**
Words and music by Mike Watt.
tHUNDERSPIEL, 1991/Bug Music.
Introduced by fIREHOSE on *Flyin' the Flannel* (Columbia, 91).
  Veteran of legendary underground favorites, The Minutemen.

**FMUSA** (English)
Words and music by Andy Gill.
Copyright Control, 1991.
Introduced by Gang of Four on *Mall* (Polydor, 91).

**Fooled Around and Fell in Love**
Words and music by Elvin Bishop.
Crabshaw Music, 1976.
Revived by Henry Lee Summer in the film and on the soundtrack
  album *Queen's Logic* (Epic, 91).

**For My Broken Heart**
Words and music by Liz Hengber and Keith Palmer.
Starstruck Writers Group.
Best-selling record by Reba McEntire from *For My Broken Heart*
  (MCA, 91).

**For My Mary**
Music by Charles Strouse, words by Stephen Schwartz.
Charles Strouse Music, 1986/Grey Dog Music.
Revived in *Rags* (91).

**Forever My Lady**
Words and music by DeVante Swing and Al B. Sure.
EMI-April Music Inc., 1991/Across 110th Street/Deswing Mob/Al
  B. Sure International.
Best-selling record by Jodeci from *Forever My Lady* (MCA, 91).

**Forever Together**
Words and music by Randy Travis and Alan Jackson.
Sometimes You Win, 1991/All Nations Music/Seventh Son Music
  Inc./Mattie Ruth.
Best-selling record by Randy Travis from *High Lonesome* (Warner
  Bros., 91).

**Forever's as Far as I'll Go**
Words and music by Mike Reid.
Almo Music Corp., 1990/Brio Blues.
Best-selling record by Alabama from *Pass It on Down* (RCA, 90).

**Freedom '90** (English)
Words and music by George Michael.
Morrison Leahy, England, 1990/Chappell & Co., Ltd., London,
    England.
Best-selling record by George Michael from *Listen Without Prejudice,
    Vol. 1* (Columbia, 90).

**From a Distance**
Words and music by Julie Gold.
Julie Gold's Music, 1987/Wing & Wheel/Irving Music Inc.
Best-selling record by Bette Midler from *Some People's Lives* (Atlantic,
    90).

**Fun to Be Perfect**
Words and music by Julie Gold.
Julie Gold's Music, 1991/Irving Music Inc.
Introduced by Julie Gold on *Fast Folk Musical Magazine* (Fast Folk,
    91).

# G

**Get a Leg Up**
Words and music by John Mellencamp.
Full Keel, 1991.
Best-selling record by John Mellencamp from *Whenever We Wanted*
(Mercury, 91).

**Get Here**
Words and music by Brenda Russell.
WB Music Corp., 1990/Rutland Road.
Best-selling record by Oleta Adams from *Circle of One* (Fontana, 90).

**Gett Off**
Words and music by Prince & the New Power Generation.
Controversy Music, 1991/WB Music Corp.
Introduced by Prince and the New Power Generation on *Diamonds
and Pearls* (Paisley Park, 91).

**The Gift of Life**
Words and music by Desmond Child.
EMI-April Music Inc., 1991/Desmobile Music Co.
Introduced by Desmond Child on *Discipline* (Elektra, 91).

**Give Peace a Chance**
Words and music by John Lennon and Yoko Ono, words by Sean
Lennon.
Lenono Music, 1969.
Revived by Sean Lennon (Virgin, 91). The son of Yoko Ono and the
late Beatle is joined on this charity project by Lenny Kravitz,
Bonnie Raitt, Tom Petty, Peter Gabriel, Hammer, and L.L. Cool J
on behalf of the John Lennon Greening of the World Foundation.
Released on the eve of the Gulf War as an anti-war anthem in
protest of the United States' involvement.

**Go Back to the Woods**
Words and music by Robbie Robertson and Bruce Hornsby.
Medicine Hat Music, 1991/EMI-April Music Inc.
Introduced by Robbie Robertson on *Storyville* (Geffen, 91).

**God Loves a Drunk** (English)
Words and music by Richard Thompson.
Beeswing Music, 1991.
Introduced by Richard Thompson on *Rumor and Sigh* (Capitol, 91).

**Going Out Tonight**
Words and music by John Jennings and Mary Chapin Carpenter.
EMI-April Music Inc., 1990/Getarealjob Music/Obie Diner/Bug
    Music.
Introduced by Mary Chapin Carpenter on *Shooting Straight in the
    Dark* (Columbia, 90).

**Gonna Make You Sweat**
Words and music by Rob Clivilles and Freedom Williams.
Virgin Music, Inc., 1991/Cole-Clivilles.
Best-selling record by C & C Music Factory Featuring Freedom
    Williams from *Gonna Make You Sweat* (Columbia, 91).

**Good Vibrations**
Words and music by Donnie Wahlberg, Mark Wahlberg, and Spice.
WB Music Corp., 1991/Donnie D./Marky Mark/Ayesha.
Best-selling record by Marky Mark and the Funky Bunch and Loleatta
    Holloway from *Music for the People* (Interscope, 91).

**Gotta Have You**
Words and music by Stevie Wonder.
Steveland Morris Music, 1991.
Introduced by Stevie Wonder in the film and on the soundtrack *Jungle
    Fever* (Motown, 91). Nominated for a Grammy Award, Best-selling
    record Written for a Film.

**Growin' Up in the Hood**
Music by Terry Allen, Andre Manuel, and Joe Simon, words by
    Aaron Tyler.
Anna Gate, 1991/Warner-Tamerlane Publishing Corp./Grandma's
    Hands.
Introduced by Compton's Most Wanted in the film and on the
    soundtrack *Boyz N the Hood*. Also featured on *Straight Checkn Em*
    (Orpheus/Epic, 91).

**Gun Song**
Words and music by Stephen Sondheim.

Revelation Music Publishing Corp., 1990/Rilting Music Inc.
Introduced by Victor Garber, Jonathan Hadary, and Terence Mann in
   *Assassins* and featured on original cast album (RCA, 91).

**Gypsy Woman (She's Homeless)**
Words and music by Crystal Waters and Neil Conway.
Basement Boys, 1991/Polygram International.
Best-selling record by Crystal Waters from *Surprise* (Mercury, 91).
   Addressing one of urban America's most pressing problems.

# H

**Hangar 18**
Words and music by Dave Mustaine.
Mustaine Music, 1990/Theory Music/Screen Gems-EMI Music Inc.
Revived by Megadeth on *Maximum Megadeth* (Capitol, 91).

**Happiness Is a Warm Gun**
Words and music by John Lennon and Paul McCartney.
Northern Music Co., 1968/Maclen Music Inc.
Revived by World Party on *Thank You World* (Chrysalis, 91).

**A Heart Is a House for Love**
Words and music by Tristan Sigerson, Davitt Sigerson, and Bob
    Thiele.
TCF, 1990/EMI-April Music Inc./SMICSMAC/Behind Bars.
Introduced by The Dells in the film and on the soundtrack album *The
    Five Heartbeats* (Virgin, 91).

**Heat of the Moment**
Words and music by Babyface (pseudonym for Kenny Edmunds) and
    L. A. Reid (pseudonym for Antonio Reid).
Hip-Trip Music Co./Kear Music.
Best-selling record by After 7 from the album *Nights Like This* (Virgin,
    91).

**Heaven**
Words and music by Julie Gold.
Julie Gold's Music, 1988/Irving Music Inc.
Introduced by Nanci Griffith on *Late Night Grande Hotel* (MCA, 91).

**Here I Am (Come and Take Me)** (English)
Words and music by Warren Hodges.
Irving Music Inc., 1973/Al Green Music Inc.
Revived by UB40 from *Labour of Love II* (Virgin, 89).

**Here We Are**
Words and music by Beth Neilsen Chapman.
Warner-Chappell Music, 1990/Macy Place Music/Benefit.
Best-selling record by Alabama from *Pass It on Down* (RCA, 90).

**Here We Go**
Words and music by Rob Clivilles and Freedom Williams.
Virgin Music, Inc., 1991/Cole-Clivilles/RGB-Dome.
Best-selling record by C & C Music Factory featuring Freedom
    Williams and Zelma Davis from *Gonna Make You Sweat* (Columbia,
    91).

**Here's a Quarter (Call Someone Who Cares)**
Words and music by Travis Tritt.
Sony Tree, 1991/Post Oak/RGB-Dome.
Best-selling record by Travis Tritt from *It's All About to Change*
    (Warner Bros., 91). Nominated for a Grammy Award, Best Country
    Song of the Year .

**Heroes and Friends**
Words and music by Don Schlitz and Randy Travis.
Sometimes You Win, 1990/All Nations Music/Don Schlitz
    Music/Almo Music Corp.
Best-selling record by Randy Travis from *Heroes and Friends* (Warner
    Bros., 90).

**Hey Donna**
Words and music by Carl Sturken and Evan Rogers.
Bayjun Beat, 1991.
Best-selling record by Rythm Syndicate from *Rythm Syndicate*
    (Impact, 91).

**High Enough**
Words and music by Ted Nugent, Tommy Shaw, and Jack Blades.
Ranch Rock, 1990/Warner-Tamerlane Publishing Corp./Tranquility
    Base Songs/WB Music Corp./Broadhead.
Best-selling record by Damn Yankees from *Damn Yankees* (Warner
    Bros., 90).

**Highwire** (English)
Words and music by Mick Jagger and Keith Richards.
Promopub BV, 1991.
Introduced by The Rolling Stones on *Flashpoint* (Rolling Stones, 91).

**Hillbilly Girl**
Words and music by Greg Brown.

Brown/Feldman, 1990.
Introduced by Greg Brown on *Down in There* (Red House, 90).

**Hold You Tight**
Words and music by William Hammond, Tuhin Roy, and Jake Smith.
Kallman Music, Inc., 1991/One-Two.
Best-selling record by Tara Kemp from *Tara Kemp* (Giant, 91).

**Hole Hearted**
Music by Nuno Bettencourt, words by Gary Cherone.
Funky Metal, 1990/Almo Music Corp.
Best-selling record by Extreme from *Pornograffiti II* (A & M, 90).

**Holy Wars**
Words and music by Matthew Sweet.
EMI-Blackwood Music Inc., 1989/Charm Trap Music.
Introduced by Matthew Sweeet on *Girlfriend* (BMG, 91).

**How Can I Ease the Pain**
Words and music by Narada Michael Walden and Lisa Fischer.
Gratitude Sky Music, Inc., 1991/Melonie/MCA Music.
Best-selling record by Lisa Fischer from *So Intense* (Elektra, 91).
  Nominated for a Grammy Award, Best Rhythm 'n' Blues Song of
  the Year .

**How Can You Expect to Be Taken Seriously** (English)
Words and music by Chris Lowe and Neil Tennant.
Cage Music Ltd., England, 1990/10 Music Ltd., England.
Introduced by Pet Shop Boys on *Behaviour* (EMI, 90).

**How to Kill a Radio Consultant**
Words by Carlton Ridenhour, Stuart Robertz, Gary G. Wiz, and
  Cerwin Dopper.
Def American Songs, 1991.
Introduced by Public Enemy on *Apocalypse '91...The Enemy Strikes
  Back* (Def Jam/Columbia, 91).

**Human Being**
Words and music by David Johansen and Johnny Thunders.
Seldak Music Corp., 1974/Haverstraw.
Revival of The New York Dolls on *The Groups of Wrath* (TVT, 91).
  Seminal glam-rock band on the New York City scene, originally on
  the album *Too Much Too Soon* (74).

**Hurt Me Bad (in a Real Good Way)**
Words and music by Deborah Allen and Rafe Van Hoy.

Posey Publishing, 1991/Rockin' R.
Best-selling record by Patty Loveless from *Up Against My Heart* (MCA, 91).

# I

**I Adore Mi Amor**
Words and music by Hamza Lee and Color Me Badd.
Me Good, 1991/Azmah Eel.
Best-selling record by Color Me Badd from *C.M.B.* (Giant, 91).

**I Am a Simple Man**
Words and music by Walt Aldridge.
Rick Hall Music, 1991.
Best-selling record by Ricky Van Shelton from *Backroads* (Columbia, 91).

**I Can't Wait Another Minute**
Words and music by Eric Foster White.
Zomba Enterprises, Inc., 1991/4MW.
Best-selling record by Hi-Five from *Hi-Five* (Jive, 91).

**I Could Learn to Love You**
Words and music by Ashley Cleveland.
Warner-Tamerlane Publishing Corp., 1991.
Introduced by Ashley Cleveland on *Big Town* (Atlantic, 91).

**I Couldn't See You Leavin'**
Words and music by Ronnie Scarfe and Rory Bourke.
Songs of Polygram, 1990/Partner/Polygram International/Songs de Burgo.
Best-selling record by Conway Twity from *Crazy in Love* (RCA, 90).

**(Everything I Do) I Do It for You (from *Robin Hood*)**
Words and music by Bryan Adams, Robert John "Mutt" Lange, and Michael Kamen.
Almo Music Corp., 1991/Badams/Zomba Enterprises, Inc./Zachary Creek.
Best-selling record by Bryan Adams from the film and soundtrack album *Robin Hood: Prince of Thieves* (Morgan Creek, 91).

Nominated for Grammy Awards, Best Record of the Year and Best Song of the Year , and won a Grammy Award, Best Song Written for a Film. Also nominated for an Academy Award, Best Original Song.

### I Don't Wanna Cry
Words and music by Mariah Carey and Narada Michael Walden.
Vision of Love Songs Inc., 1991/Sony Songs/Gratitude Sky Music, Inc.
Best-selling record by Mariah Carey from *Mariah Carey* (Columbia, 90).

### I Don't Wanna Lose Your Love
Words and music by Bruce Hawes and Wanda Hutchinson.
EMI-Blackwood Music Inc., 1976/Pam Jo Keen.
Best-selling record by B Angie B from *B Angie B* (Bust It, 91).

### I Feel So Good (English)
Words and music by Richard Thompson.
Beeswing Music, 1991.
Introduced by Richard Thompson on *Rumor and Sigh* (Capitol, 91).

### I Go to Pieces
Words and music by Del Shannon.
Bug Music, 1964/Mole Hole Music/Unichappell Music Inc.
Revival of Del Shannon recording on *Rock On* (Bug/MCA, 91).

### I Have My Moments
Words by John Popper, music by Chan Kinchla.
Blues Traveler, 1991/Irving Music Inc.
Introduced by Blues Traveler on *Travelers & Thieves* (A & M, 91).

### I Hear They Smoke the Barbecue
Words and music by Eric Drew Feldman, Jim Jones, Scott Krauss, Tony Maimone, and David Thomas.
Phonogram, 1991/Polygram Music Publishing Inc.
Introduced by Pere Ubu on *Worlds in Collision* (Fontana, 91).

### I Like the Way (The Kissing Game)
Words and music by Teddy Riley, Bernard Belle, and David Way.
Zomba Enterprises, Inc., 1990/WB Music Corp./B. Funk/Donril Music.
Best-selling record by Hi-Five from *Hi-Five* (Jive/RCA, 90).

**I Love Your Smile**
Words and music by Narada Michael Walden, Shanice Wilson, Sylvester Jackson, and Jarvis La Rue Baker.
Shanice 4U, 1991/Gratitude Sky Music, Inc.
Best-selling record by Shanice from *Inner Child* (Motown, 91).

**I Misunderstood** (English)
Words and music by Richard Thompson.
Beeswing Music, 1991.
Best-selling record by Richard Thompson on *Rumor and Sigh* (Capitol, 91).

**I Saw Red**
Words and music by Jani Lane.
Virgin Songs, 1990/Dick Dragon Music.
Best-selling record by Warrant from *Cherry Pie* (Columbia, 90).

**I Touch Myself** (Australian)
Words and music by Billy Steinberg, Tom Kelly, Christina Amphlett, and Mark McEntee.
EMI Songs (Australia), Australia/Billy Steinberg Music, 1990/Denise Barry Music/EMI-Blackwood Music Inc.
Best-selling record by Divinyls from *Divinyls* (Virgin, 91).

**I Wanna Be a Boss**
Words and music by Stan Ridgway.
Mondo Spartacus Music, 1991/Illegal Songs, Inc./Criterion Music Corp.
Introduced by by Stan Ridgway on *Partyball* (Geffen, 91).

**I Wanna Be Like Mike**
Words by Jay Johnson, Sir Jam, and Keith Evans, music by Steve Shafer, Ira Antelis, and Bernie Pitzel.
Quaker Oats, Inc., 1991.
Introduced by Teknoe (A & M, 91).

**I Wanna Be Your Boyfriend**
Words and music by Ramones.
Taco Tunes Inc., 1975/Bleu Disque Music.
Revival of The Ramones on *The Groups of Wrath* (TVT, 91).

**I Wanna Sex You Up (from *New Jack City*)**
Words and music by Dr. Freeze (pseudonym for Elliot Straite).
Hip Hop, 1990/Hi-Frost.
Best-selling record Color Me Badd from the film and soundtrack album *New Jack City* (Giant, 91). Nominated for a Grammy Award, Best Rhythm 'n' Blues Song of the Year .

**I Wish You Were Her** (English)
Words and music by Billy Bragg.
Utilitarian Music (England), 1991.
Introduced by Billy Bragg on *Don't Try This at Home* (Elektra, 91).

**I Wonder Why**
Words and music by Greg Ballard and Curtis Stigers.
Sony Tunes, 1991/C. Montrose S./Aerostation Corp./MCA Music.
Best-selling record by Curtis Stigers from *Curtis Stigers* (Arista, 91).

**I'd Love You All Over Again**
Words and music by Alan Jackson.
Mattie Ruth, 1990/Seventh Son Music Inc.
Best-selling record by Alan Jackson from *Here in the Real World* (Arista, 90).

**Iesha**
Words and music by Dallas Austin and Michael Bivins.
Diva One, 1991/Diva 1 Music.
Best-selling record by Another Bad Creation from *Coolin' at the Playground Ya' Know!* (Motown, 91).

**If I Know Me**
Words and music by Dean Dillon and Pam Belford.
Music Corp. of America, 1991/Jessie Joe/Dixie Stars/Brass & Chance.
Best-selling record by George Strait from *Chill of an Early Fall* (MCA, 91).

**If It's Over**
Music by Carole King, words and music by Mariah Carey.
Lushmole, London, England/M. Carey Songs, 1991/Sony Music Publishing.
Introduced by Mariah Carey on *Emotions* (Columbia, 91).

**If She Knew What She Wants**
Words and music by Jules Shear.
Funzalo Music, 1986/Juters Publishing Co.
Revived by Jules Shear on *Unplug This* (Polygram, 91).

**If the Devil Danced (in Empty Pockets)**
Words and music by Ken Spooner and Kim Williams.
Texas Wedge, 1990/Sony Cross Keys Publishing Co. Inc.
Best-selling record by Joe Diffie from *A Thousand Winding Roads* (Epic, 90).

**If We Never Meet Again**
Words and music by Jules Shear.

Juters Publishing Co., 1988/Music Corp. of America.
Introduced by Roger McGuinn on *Back from Rio* (Arista, 90).

**If You Don't Start Drinking (I'm Gonna Leave)**
Words and music by George Thorogood.
Del Sounds Music, 1991.
Introduced by George Thorogood and the Destroyers on *Boogie People* (EMI, 91).

**If You Needed Somebody**
Words and music by Brian Howe and Terry Thomas.
Warner-Chappell Music, 1990/TJT/Phantom.
Best-selling record by Bad Company from *Holy Water* (Atco, 90).

**If You Want Me To**
Words and music by Lonnie Williams and Joe Diffie.
Songwriters Ink, 1990/Forrest Hills Music Inc.
Best-selling record by Joe Diffie from *A Thousand Winding Roads* (Epic, 90).

**I'll Be by Your Side**
Words and music by Stevie B. and Dadgel Atabay.
SHR, 1990/Mya-T.
Best-selling record by Stevie B. from *Love & Emotion* (LMR, 90).

**I'll Be There**
Words and music by The Escape Club.
Love Pump, 1991/Warner-Chappell Music/Warner-Tamerlane Publishing Corp.
Best-selling record by The Escape Club from *Dollars and Sex* (Atlantic, 91).

**I'll Give All My Love to You**
Words and music by Keith Sweat and Brian Wooten.
WB Music Corp., 1990/E/A/Sony Tunes/Keith Sweat/Maestro B.
Best-selling record by Keith Sweat from *I'll Give All My Love to You* (Vintertainment, 90).

**I'll Take You There**
Words and music by Alvertis Isbele.
Irving Music Inc., 1972.
Best-selling record by Bebe and Cece Winans featuring Mavis Staples from *Different Lifestyles* (Capitol, 91). Nominated for a Grammy Award, Best Rhythm 'n' Blues Song of the Year .

**I'm Dreamin' (from *New Jack City*)**
Words and music by Stanley Brown.

H-Naja, 1990/La Sab.
Best-selling record by Christopher Williams from the soundtrack album and film *New Jack City* (Giant, 91).

**I'm Not in Love** (English)
Words and music by Graham Gouldman and Eric Stewart.
Man-Ken Music Ltd., 1975.
Revived by Will to Power from *Journey Home* (Epic, 91).

**I'm Not Romantic**
Words and music by Phranc.
Folkswim, 1991.
Introduced by Phranc on *Positively Phranc* (Island, 91).

**I'm on Your Side**
Words and music by Billy Steinberg and Tom Kelly.
Billy Steinberg Music, 1990/Denise Barry Music.
Introduced by Divinyls on *Divinyls* (Virgin, 91).

**I'm Talking to My Pal**
Words by Lorenz Hart, music by Richard Rodgers.
Chappell & Co., Inc., 1940, 1951, 1962.
Revived by Mandy Patinkin on *Dress Casual* (CBS, 90). Written for *Pal Joey* but dropped before opening night.

**I'm Worthy of Your Love**
Words and music by Stephen Sondheim.
Revelation Music Publishing Corp., 1990/Rilting Music Inc.
Introduced by Greg Germann and Annie Golden in *Assassins* as John Hinckley and Lynette "Squeaky" Fromme. Revived on the original cast album (RCA, 91).

**I'm Your Baby Tonight**
Words and music by L. A. Reid (pseudonym for Antonio Reid) and Babyface (pseudonym for Kenny Edmunds).
Kear Music, 1990/CBS/Epic/Solar.
Best-selling record by Whitney Houston from *I'm Your Baby Tonight* (Arista, 90).

**Impulsive**
Words and music by Steve Kipner and Cliff Magness.
EMI-April Music Inc., 1989/Stephen A. Kipner/WB Music Corp./Magnified.
Best-selling record by Wilson Phillips from *Wilson Phillips* (SBK, 90).

**In a Different Light**
Words and music by Bob McDill, Bucky Jones, and Dickie Lee.

PolyGram Records Inc., 1991/Ranger Bob Music/Cross Keys
Publishing Co., Inc./Polygram Songs.
Best-selling record by Doug Stone on *Doug Stone* (Epic, 91).

**Instant Karma Coffee House**
Words and music by David Grover.
EMI-Blackwood Music Inc., 1991/Da Braddah's.
Introduced by Loud Sugar on *Loud Sugar* (SBK, 91).

**Into a Mall**
Words and music by Don Henry.
Sony Cross Keys Publishing Co. Inc., 1985.
Performed by Don Henry on *Wild in the Backyard* (Sony, 91).

**It Ain't Over Til It's Over**
Words and music by Lenny Kravitz.
Miss Bessie, 1991.
Best-selling record by Lenny Kravitz from *Mama Said* (Virgin, 91).

**It Hit Me Like a Hammer** (American-English)
Words and music by Robert John "Mutt" Lange and Huey Lewis.
Zomba Enterprises, Inc., 1991/Hulex Music.
Introduced by Huey Lewis and the News on *Hard at Play* (Chrysalis,
91).

**It Should've Been You**
Words and music by Teddy Pendergrass and Terry Price.
Ted-On Music, 1991.
Best-selling record by Teddy Pendergrass from *Truly Blessed* (Elektra,
91).

**It Takes Time**
Words and music by Fred Smith and Patti Smith.
Stratium Music Inc., 1991/Druse Music Inc.
Introduced by Patti Smith and Fred Smith in the film and on the
soundtrack LP *Until the End of the World* (Warner Bros., 91).

**It's Been a Long Time**
Words and music by Steven Van Zandt.
Little Jake, 1991.
Introduced by Southside Johnny & The Asbury Jukes on *Better Days*
(Impact, 91).

**It's Love**
Words and music by King's X.
Jetydosa, 1991/Ackee Music Inc.
Introduced by King's X on *Faith Hope Love* (Megaforce, 91).

**It's So Hard to Say Goodbye to Yesterday**
Words and music by Freddie Perren and Christine Yarian.
Jobete Music Co., Inc., 1991.
Best-selling record by Boyz II Men from *Cooleyhighharmony* (Motown, 91).

**I've Been Thinking About You** (English)
Words and music by Henshall, George Chandler, and Jimmy Chambers.
Warner-Tamerlane Publishing Corp., 1991.
Best-selling record by Londonbeat from *In the Blood* (Radioactive, 91).

**I've Got That Old Feeling**
Words and music by Sidney Cox.
Sidney Lawrence Company, 1990.
Introduced by Alison Krauss on *I've Got That Old Feeling* (Rounder, 90).

# J

**Jet City Woman**
Words and music by Chris DeGarmo and Geoff Tate.
Tri Ryche, 1991/Screen Gems-EMI Music Inc.
Introduced by Queensryche on *Empire* (EMI, 91).

**John Deere Tractor**
Words and music by L. J. Hammond.
Rada Dara Music, 1983.
Best-selling record by The Judds from *Love Can Build a Bridge*
    (RCA/Curb, 90).

**Joyride** (Swedish)
Words and music by Per Gessle.
Jimmie Fun, Sweden, 1991/EMI-Blackwood Music Inc.
Best-selling record by Roxette from *Joyride* (EMI, 91).

**Jungle Fever**
Words and music by Stevie Wonder.
Steveland Morris Music, 1991.
Introduced by Stevie Wonder in the film and on the soundtrack *Jungle
    Fever* (Motown, 91). Nominated for a Grammy Award, Best Song
    Written for a Film.

**Just Another Dream**
Words and music by Cathy Dennis and Denny Poku.
Colgems-EMI Music Inc., 1990/EMI-Blackwood Music Inc.
Best-selling record by Cathy Dennis from *Move to This* (Polydor, 90).

**Just the Way It Is, Baby**
Words and music by Phil Solem and Denny Wilde.

WB Music Corp., 1991/Warner-Tamerlane Publishing Corp./Tiger God.

Best-selling record by The Rembrandts from *The Rembrandts* (Atco, 91).

**Justify My Love**
Words and music by Madonna Ciccone and Lenny Kravitz.
Miss Bessie, 1990/Bleu Disque Music/WB Music Corp./Webo Girl.
Best-selling record by Madonna from *The Immaculate Collection* (Warner Bros., 90).

**Juvenile Delinquintz**
Words by Lamont Lake and Norman Rogers.
Shocklee, 1991.
Introduced by Terminator X on *Terminator X and the Valley of the Jeep Beets* (P.R.O. Division/Columbia, 91).

# K

**Katy Says Today Is the Best Day of My Whole Entire Life**
Words and music by Christine Lavin.
Flip-a-Jig, 1991.
Introduced by Christine Lavin on *Compass* (Philo, 91).

**Keep Coming Back**
Words and music by Richard Marx.
Chi-Boy, 1991.
Best-selling record by Richard Marx from *Rush Street* (Capitol, 91).

**Keep It Between the Lines**
Words and music by Russell Smith and Kathy Louvin.
MCA Music, 1991/Tillis.
Best-selling record by Ricky Van Shelton from *Backroads* (Columbia, 91).

**Keep Your Distance** (English)
Words and music by Richard Thompson.
Beeswing Music, 1991.
Best-selling record by Richard Thompson on *Rumor and Sigh* (Capitol, 91).

**The Kid Inside**
Words and music by Craig Carnelia.
Carnelia Music, 1982/A. Schroeder International Ltd.
Revived by Barry Manilow on *Showstoppers* (Arista, 91).

**King of the Hill**
Words and music by Roger McGuinn and Tom Petty.
McGuinn Music, 1990/Gone Gator Music.
Introduced by Roger McGuinn on *Back from Rio* (Arista, 90).

**Kiss the Girl**
Music by Alan Menken, words by Howard Ashman.

Walt Disney Music Co., 1988/Wonderland Music Co., Inc.
Revived by Soul II Soul on *Simply Mad About the Mouse* (Columbia, 91).

### Kissing You

Words and music by Keith Washington, Marsha Jenkins, and Rodney Shelton.
EMI-April Music Inc., 1991/K-Shreve/Market Music/Full Keel/JRM.
Best-selling record by Keith Washington from *Make Time for Love* (Qwest, 91).

# L

**Last Chance**
Words and music by John Mellencamp.
Full Keel, 1991.
Introduced by John Mellencamp on *Whenever We Wanted* (Mercury, 91).

**The Last 40 Years**
Words and music by Craig Carnelia.
Carnelia Music, 1975/A. Schroeder International Ltd.
Revived by Craig Carnelia on *Pictures in the Hall* (Original Cast, 91).

**The Last Time I Had Autumn**
Words and music by Fred Small.
Pine Barrens Music, 1991.
Introduced by Fred Small on *Jaguar* (Flying Fish, 91).

**Late Night Grande Hotel**
Words and music by Nanci Griffith.
Ponder Heart Music, 1991/Irving Music Inc.
Introduced by Nanci Griffith on *Late Night Grande Hotel* (MCA, 91).

**Latifah's Had It Up to Here**
Words by Queen Latifah (pseudonym for D. Owens), music by Vinnie Brown, Kier Gist, and Anthony Criss.
T-Boy, 1991/Queen Latifah/Naughty.
Introduced by Queen Latifah on *Nature of a Sista* (Tommy Boy, 91).

**Leap of Faith**
Words and music by Lionel Cartwright.
Warner-Tamerlane Publishing Corp., 1991/Long Run Music Co., Inc.
Best-selling record by Lionel Cartwright from *Chasin' the Sun* (MCA, 91).

**Learning to Fly**
Words and music by Tom Petty and Jeff Lynne.

Gone Gator Music, 1991/EMI-April Music Inc.
Introduced by Tom Petty on *Into the Great Wide Open* (MCA, 91). Nominated for a Grammy, Best Rock Song of the Year.

**Let the Beat Hit 'Em**
Words and music by David Cole, Rob Clivilles, Alan Friedman, and Duran Ramos.
Virgin Music, Inc., 1991/Cole-Clivilles.
Best-selling record by Lisa Lisa and Cult Jam from *Straight Outa Hell's Kitchen* (Columbia, 91).

**Let's Chill**
Words and music by Teddy Riley, Bernard Belle, and Keith Sweat.
Zomba Enterprises, Inc., 1990/B. Funk/WB Music Corp./Donril Music.
Best-selling record by Guy from *The Future* (Uptown, 90).

**Let's Talk Dirty in Hawaiian**
Words and music by Fred Kolker and John Prine.
Lucrative, 1987/Grandma Annie Music/Spoondevil/Bug Music.
Revived by Wild Jimbos on *Wild Jimbos* (RCA, 91).

**Lies** (English)
Words and music by Ian Dench.
WB Music Corp., 1991.
Best-selling record by EMF from *Schubert Dip* (EMI, 91).

**Lift Me Up** (English)
Words and music by Trevor Rabin and Chris Squire.
Affirmative, 1991/Warner-Tamerlane Publishing Corp.
Introduced by Yes on *Union* (Arista, 91).

**Lily Was Here**
Words and music by David A. Stewart.
D 'N' A, 1991/Careers Music Inc.
Best-selling record by David A. Stewart featuring Candy Dulfer from *Saxuality* (Arista, 91).

**Lily's Eyes**
Music by Lucy Simon, words by Marsha Norman.
Calogie Music, 1991/ABCDE/WB Music Corp.
Introduced by Mandy Patinkin and Robert Westenberg in *Secret Garden* and on original cast album (Columbia, 91).

**Lines in the Sand**
Words and music by Randy Newman.

Warner-Tamerlane Publishing Corp., 1991/Randy Newman Music.
Introduced by Randy Newman (Warner Bros., 91). Relating to the war
   with Iraq.

**Live and Let Die**
Words and music by Paul McCartney and Linda McCartney.
MPL Communications Inc., 1973/EMI Unart Catalogue.
Revived by Guns N' Roses on *Use Your Illusion I* (Geffen, 91).

**Living with the Law**
Words and music by Chris Whitley.
Reata Publishing Inc., 1991/Srete/WB Music Corp.
Introduced by Chris Whitley on *Living with the Law* (Columbia, 91).

**Look Around**
Music by Cy Coleman, words by Betty Comden and Adolph Green.
Notable Music Co., Inc., 1991/Betdolph Music.
Introduced by The Will Rogers Follies featuring Keith Carradine in
   the musical and on the LP *The Will Rogers Follies* (Columbia, 91).

**Losing My Religion**
Words and music by Walter Berry, Peter Buck, Mike Mills, and
   Michael Stipe.
Night Garden Music, 1991/Unichappell Music Inc.
Best-selling record by REM from *Out of Time* (Warner Bros., 91).
   Nominated for two Grammy Awards, Best Song of the Year and
   Best Rock Song of the Year.

**Louisiana 1927**
Words and music by Randy Newman.
Warner-Tamerlane Publishing Corp., 1974/Randy Newman Music.
Revived by Aaron Neville on *Warm Your Heart* (A & M, 91).

**Love and Understanding**
Words and music by Diane Warren.
Realsongs, 1991.
Best-selling record by Cher from *Love Hurts* (Geffen, 91).

**Love Can Build a Bridge**
Words and music by Naomi Judd, John Jarvis, and Paul Overstreet.
Scarlet Moon Music, 1990.
Introduced by The Judds in *Love Can Build a Bridge* (RCA/Curb, 90).
   Won Grammy Award, Best Country Song of the Year.

**Love in the Rain**
Words and music by Lamont Dozier.

45

Beau Di O Do Music, 1991/Warner-Tamerlane Publishing Corp.
Introduced by Lamont Dozier on *Inside Seduction* (Atlantic, 91).

### Love Is a Wonderful Thing
Words and music by Michael Bolton and Andy Goldmark.
Mr. Bolton's Music, 1991/Warner-Tamerlane Publishing
  Corp./Nonpariel Music/WB Music Corp.
Best-selling record by Michael Bolton from *Time, Love and Tenderness* (Columbia, 91).

### Love Makes Things Happen
Words and music by Babyface (pseudonym for Kenny Edmunds) and
  L. A. Reid (pseudonym for Antonio Reid).
Kear Music, 1990/Sony Epic/Solar.
Best-selling record by Pebbles from *Alwyas* (MCA, 90).

### Love Me
Words and music by Skip Ewing and Max T. Barnes.
Acuff-Rose Publications Inc., 1991/Two-Sons Music/WB Music
  Corp.
Best-selling record by Colin Raye from *All I Can Be* (Epic, 91).

### Love of a Lifetime
Words and music by Bill Leverty and C. J. Snare.
Sony Tunes, 1991/Wocka Wocka.
Best-selling record by Firehouse from *Firehouse* (Epic, 91).

### Love Takes Time
Words and music by Mariah Carey and Ben Marguiles.
Vision of Love Songs Inc., 1990/Been Jammin' Music.
Best-selling record by Mariah Carey from *Mariah Carey* (Columbia, 90).

### Love Will Never Do (Without You)
Words and music by James Harris, III and Terry Lewis.
Flyte Tyme Tunes, 1989.
Best-selling record by Janet Jackson from *Rhythm Nation 1814* (A & M, 89).

### Loving Blind
Words and music by Clint Black.
Howlin' Hits Music, 1990.
Best-selling record by Clint Black from *Put Yourself in My Shoes* (RCA, 90).

### Luck of the Draw
Words and music by Paul Brady.

Rondor Music Inc., 1991/Almo Music Corp.
Introduced by Bonnie Raitt on *Luck of the Draw* (Capitol, 91).

**Lying**
Words and music by Sam Phillips.
Eden Bridge Music, 1991.
Introduced by Sam Phillips on *Cruel Inventions* (Virgin, 91).

# M

**Main Course**
Words and music by Paul Laurence.
MCA Music, 1990/Bush Burnin' Music.
Best-selling record by Freddie Jackson from *Do Me Again* (Capitol, 90).

**Mama Said Knock You Out**
Words and music by Marlon Williams and James Todd Smith.
Marley Marl, 1991/L.L. Cool J Music/Def Jam.
Best-selling record by L.L. Cool J from *Mama Said Knock You Out* (Def Jam, 91).

**Maybe I Mean Yes**
Words and music by Holly Dunn, Chris Waters, and Tom Shapiro.
Careers-BMG, 1991/South Heart/Edge o' the Woods/Kinetic Diamond/Moline Valley.
Introduced by Holly Dunn on *Milestones, Greatest Hits* (Warner Bros., 91). Song drew a lot of heat for its confusion of date rape with seduction.

**Meet in the Middle**
Words and music by Chapin Hartford, Jim Foster, and Don Pfrimmer.
Sony Tree, 1991/Electric Mule/Zomba Enterprises, Inc.
Best-selling record by Diamond Rio from *Diamond Rio* (Arista, 91).

**Men**
Words and music by Gladys Knight, Attala Zane Giles, and Cornelius Mims.
Shakeji, 1991/Captain Z/Welbeck Music Corp./Cornelios Carlos/MCA Music.
Best-selling record by Gladys Knight from *Good Women* (MCA, 91).

**Mercy Mercy Me (The Ecology)/I Want You**
Words and music by Marvin Gaye, Arthur Ross, and Leon Ware.
Jobete Music Co., Inc., 1971/Almo Music Corp.
Revived by Robert Palmer from *Don't Explain* (EMI, 91).

**Michigan Water**
Words and music by Jellyroll Morton, music by Luther Henderson,
    words by Susan Birkenhead.
Edwin H. Morris, 1991.
Performed by Mary Bond Davis in the musical *Jelly's Last Jam* at the
    Mark Taper Forum in Los Angeles (91), due for Broadway in 1992.

**Miles Away**
Words and music by Paul Taylor.
Virgin Songs, 1990/Small Hope Music/Paul Taylor.
Best-selling record by Winger from *In the Heart of the Young*
    (Atlantic, 90).

**Miracle**
Words and music by L. A. Reid (pseudonym for Antonio Reid) and
    Babyface (pseudonym for Kenny Edmunds).
Kear Music, 1990/Sony Epic/Solar.
Best-selling record by Whitney Houston from *I'm Your Baby Tonight*
    (Arista, 90).

**Miracle (from *Young Guns II*)**
Words and music by Jon Bon Jovi.
Bon Jovi Publishing, 1990/PRI Music.
Best-selling record by Jon Bon Jovi from the film and soundtrack
    album *Young Guns II* (Mercury, 90). Also featured on *Blaze of Glory*
    (Mercury, 90).

**Mirror Mirror**
Words and music by John Jarrard and Mark Sanders.
Little Big Town Music, 1991/American Made Music/Alabama Band
    Music Co./MCA Music.
Best-selling record by Diamond Rio from *Diamond Rio* (Arista, 91).

**Miss Freelove '69** (Australian)
Words and music by Dave Faulkner.
Copyright Control, 1991.
Introduced by Hoodoo Gurus on *Kinky* (RCA, 91).

**Mr. Bad Example**
Words and music by Warren Zevon and Jorge Calderon.
Zevon Music Inc., 1991/Warner-Tamerlane Publishing
    Corp./Googiplex.
Introduced by Warren Zevon on *Mr. Bad Example* (Giant, 91).

**Mr. God**
Words and music by Don Henry.
Sony Cross Keys Publishing Co. Inc., 1986.
Performed by Don Henry on *Wild in the Backyard* (Sony, 91).

**Money Talks** (English)
Words and music by Andy Gill.
Copyright Control, 1991.
Introduced by Gang of Four on *Mall* (Polydor, 91).

**Moonchild River Song**
Words and music by Eric Andersen.
Wind and Sand Music, 1973.
Revived by Eric Andersen on *Stages: The Lost Album* (Columbia, 91).

**More Than Ever**
Words and music by Matt Nelson, Gunnar Nelson, and Mark Tanner.
Matt-Black, 1990/Gunster/EMI-April Music Inc./Otherwise
    Publishing/BMG Music.
Best-selling record by Nelson from *Love and Affection* (DGC, 90).

**More Than Words**
Music by Nuno Bettencourt, words by Gary Cherone.
Funky Metal, 1989/Almo Music Corp.
Best-selling record by Extreme from *Pornograffiti II* (A & M, 90).

**Mother Knows Best** (English)
Words and music by Richard Thompson.
Beeswing Music, 1991.
Introduced by Richard Thompson on *Rumor and Sigh* (Capitol, 91).

**The Motown Song**
Words and music by Larry John McNally.
Geffen Music, 1991/McNally/Unicity Music, Inc.
Best-selling record by Rod Stewart from *Vagabond Heart* (Warner
    Bros., 91).

**Motownphilly**
Words and music by Dallas Austin, Michael Bivins, Nathan Morris,
    and Shawn Stockman.
Diva 1 Music, 1991/Diva One/Mike Ten.
Best-selling record by Boyz II Men from *Cooleyhighharmony* (Motown,
    91).

**Moving the Goalposts** (English)
Words and music by Billy Bragg.
Utilitarian Music (England), 1991.
Introduced by Billy Bragg on *Don't Try This at Home* (Elektra, 91).

**My Big Mistake**
Words by Betty Comden and Adolph Green, music by Cy Coleman.
Notable Music Co., Inc., 1991/Betdolph Music.
Introduced by Dee Hoty in *The Will Rogers Follies* (Columbia, 91).

**My Book** (English)
Words and music by Paul Heaton and David Rotheray.
Go! Discs Ltd., England, 1991.
Introduced by The Beautiful South on *Choke* (Elektra, 91).

**My Career as a Homewrecker**
Words and music by Jonathan Richman.
Leprechaun Music, 1991/Rounder Music.
Introduced by Jonathan Richman on *Having a Party with Jonathan Richman* (Rounder, 91).

**My Love Life** (English)
Words and music by Morrissey and Mark Nevin.
Bona Relations Music, 1991/Warner-Tamerlane Publishing Corp.
Introduced by Morrissey on limited edition 12 inch LP (Sire/Reprise, 91).

**My Name Is Not Susan**
Words and music by Eric Foster White.
Zomba Enterprises, Inc., 1990/4MW.
Best-selling record by Whitney Houston from *I'm Your Baby Tonight* (Arista, 90).

**My Next Broken Heart**
Words and music by Don Cook, Ronnie Dunn, and Kix Brooks.
Sony Tree, 1991/Sony Cross Keys Publishing Co. Inc.
Best-selling record by Brooks & Dunn from *Brand New Man* (Arista, 91).

**My Own Best Friend**
Words by Fred Ebb, music by John Kander.
Fiddleback Music Publishing Co., Inc., 1991.
Introduced in the revue *And the World Goes Round* (91).

**My Special Child** (Irish)
Words and music by Sinead O'Connor.
EMI Music Publishing, Ltd., London, England/Promostraat, 1991/EMI-Blackwood Music Inc.
Introduced by Sinead O'Connor as a single (Ensign/Chrysalis, 91).

**(Love Moves in) Mysterious Ways**
Words and music by Dean Pitchford.

Ensign Music Corp., 1991/Pitchford/Snow Music.
Introduced by Julia Fordham in the film and on the soundtrack album *The Butcher's Wife*. Also on Fordham's album *Swept* (Virgin, 91).

# N

### Never Gonna Let You Down
Words and music by Brian Jackson.
Keep Your Music, 1990.
Best-selling record by Surface from *3 Deep* (Columbia, 90).

### Never Met a Man I Didn't Like
Words by Betty Comden and Adolph Green, music by Cy Coleman.
Notable Music Co., Inc., 1991/Betdolph Music.
Introduced by Keith Carradine in the musical and on the LP *The Will Rogers Follies* (Columbia, 91).

### Never Pay Musicians What They're Worth
Words and music by Erik Frandsen, Robert Hipkens, Michael Garin, and Paula Lockheart.
Introduced by Michael Garin and entire cast in *Song of Singapore* (91). This off-Broadway musical comedy was one of the season's unexpected treats.

### Never Stop
Words and music by Jan Kincaid.
London, 1991.
Best-selling record by The Brand New Heavies from *Brand New Heavies* (Delicious Vinyl, 91).

### New Coat of Paint
Words and music by Tom Waits.
Fifth Floor Music Inc., 1974.
Revived by Bob Seger on *The Fire Inside* (Capitol, 91).

### New Way (to Light Up an Old Flame)
Words and music by Lonnie Wilson and Joe Diffie.
Zomba Enterprises, Inc., 1990/Forrest Hills Music Inc.
Best-selling record by Joe Diffie from *A Thousand Winding Roads* (Epic, 90).

**1916** (English)
Words and music by Lemmy Kilmeister.
Warner-Chappell Music, 1991/Warner-Tamerlane Publishing Corp.
Introduced by Motorhead on *1916* (WTG, 91).

**1952 Vincent Black Lightning** (English)
Words and music by Richard Thompson.
Beeswing Music, 1991.
Best-selling record by Richard Thompson on *Rumor and Sigh* (Capitol,
  91).

**1963**
Words and music by Jonathan Richman.
Leprechaun Music, 1991/Rounder Music.
Introduced by Jonathan Richman on *Having a Party with Jonathan
  Richman* (Rounder, 91). Richman raps.

**No Son of Mine** (English)
Words and music by Tony Banks, Phil Collins, and Mike Rutherford.
Hidden Pun, 1991.
Best-selling record by Genesis from *We Can't Dance* (Atlantic, 91).

**No Women, No Cry** (Jamaican)
Words and music by Vincent Ford.
Bob Marley Music, Ltd., 1974.
Revived by Londonbeat on *In the Blood* (Radioactive/Anxious, 91).

**Nobody Knows**
Words and music by Eric Drew Feldman, Jim Jones, Scott Krauss,
  Tony Maimone, and David Thomas.
Phonogram, 1991/Polygram Music Publishing Inc.
Introduced by Pere Ubu on *Worlds in Collision* (Fontana, 91).

**November Rain**
Words and music by Axl Rose.
Guns N' Roses Music, 1991.
Introduced by Guns N' Roses on *Use Your Illusion I* (Geffen, 91).

**Now That We Found Love**
Words and music by Ken Gamble, Leon Huff, and Heavy D
  (pseudonym for Dwight Myers).
Warner-Tamerlane Publishing Corp., 1991.
Revived by Heavy D and the Boyz from *Peaceful Journey* (MCA, 91).

# O

**Obsession**
Words and music by Desmond Child and Burt Bacharach.
EMI-April Music Inc., 1991/Desmobile Music Co./New Hidden
   Valley Music Co.
Introduced by Desmond Child and Maria Vidal on *Discipline* (Elektra,
   91).

**Obvious Song** (English)
Words and music by Joe Jackson.
Pokazuka, 1991.
Introduced by Joe Jackson on *Laughter and Lust* (Virgin, 91).

**Oh Catherine**
Words and music by Eric Drew Feldman, Jim Jones, Scott Krauss,
   Tony Maimone, and David Thomas.
Phonogram, 1991/Polygram Music Publishing Inc.
Introduced by Pere Ubu on *Worlds in Collision* (Fontana, 91). Return
   of the proto bohemian band.

**On the Dark Side**
Words and music by John Cafferty.
Warner-Tamerlane Publishing Corp., 1983/John Cafferty Music.
Revival of John Cafferty and the Beaver Brown Band on *Eddie and the
   Cruisers: The Unreleased Tapes* (Scotie Bros, 91).

**Once in a Lifetime**
Words and music by David Byrne, Brian Eno, Chris Frantz, Tina
   Weymouth, and Jerry Harrison.
Bleu Disque Music, 1980/E.G. Music, Inc.
Revived by Big Daddy on *Cutting Their Own Groove* (Rhino, 91).

**The One and Only (from *Doc Hollywood*)**
Words and music by Nick Kershaw.

Chrysalis Music Corp., 1990.
Best-selling record by Chesney Hawkes from the film and soundtrack
   album *Doc Hollywood* (Chrysalis, 90).

## One Hand, One Heart
Words and music by Debbie Gibson.
Deborah Anne's Music, 1990.
Introduced by Debbie Gibson on *Anything Is Possible* (Warner Bros.,
   90).

## One More Try
Words and music by Timmy T.
RMI, 1990.
Best-selling record by Timmy T. from *Time After Time* (Quality, 91).
   One of the few successful independent singles of the year.

## One Part Be My Lover
Words and music by Bonnie Raitt and Michael O'Keefe.
Kokomo Music, 1991/Bob-a-Lew Songs.
Introduced by Bonnie Raitt on *Luck of the Draw* (Capitol, 91). First
   collaboration of the new husband and wife.

## Only Here for a Little While
Words and music by Wayland Holyfield and Rich Leigh.
EMI-April Music Inc., 1991/Ides of March Music Division/Lion
   Hearted Music.
Best-selling record by Billy Dean from *Young Man* (Capitol, 91).

## Only Human
Words and music by Barry Eastmond and Jeffrey Osborne.
Zomba Enterprises, Inc., 1990/Barry Eastmond Music/Almo Music
   Corp./March 9 Music.
Best-selling record by Jeffrey Osborne from *Only Human* (Arista, 90).

## Only Innocent
Words and music by Peter Himmelman.
Geffen Music, 1991/Hummasongs/WB Music Corp.
Introduced by Peter Himmelman on *From Strength to Strength* (Epic,
   91). Bob Dylan's son-in-law.

## Only the Ones We Love
Words and music by Tanita Tikarim.
Brogue Music, 1991/Warner-Tamerlane Publishing Corp.
Introduced by Tanita Tikarim on *Everybody's Angel* (Reprise, 91).

## O.P.P.
Words and music by Vinnie Brown, Kier Gist, and Anthony Criss,
   words and music by The Corporation.

Jobete Music Co., Inc./Naughty.
Best-selling record by Naughty By Nature from *Naughty By Nature* (Tommy Boy, 91). Initials stand for "Other People's Property"; based on The Jackson 5 classic "ABC."

**Optimistic**
Words and music by Gary Hines, Jimmy Jam (pseudonym for James Harris, III), Terry Lewis, and Prof. T.
Flyte Tyme Tunes, 1991.
Best-selling record by Sounds of Blackness from *The Evolution of Gospel* (Perspective, 91).

**The Other Day (Near Santa Cruz)**
Words and music by Leo Kottke.
Round Wound Sound, 1991/Bug Music.
Introduced by Leo Kottke on *Great Big Boy* (Private Music, 91). More vocalizing from the virtuoso guitarist.

**The Other Side of Summer** (English)
Words and music by Declan MacManus.
Plangent Visions Music, Inc., London, England, 1991.
Introduced by Elvis Costello on *Mighty Like a Rose* (Columbia, 91). Typically caustic wordplay.

**Our Frank** (English)
Words and music by Morrissey and Mark Nevin.
Warner-Chappell Music, 1991/Warner-Tamerlane Publishing Corp./Copyright Control.
Introduced by Morrissey on *Kill Uncle* (Sire/Reprise, 91).

**Outbound Plane**
Words and music by Nanci Griffith and Tom Russell.
Wing & Wheel, 1987/Bug Music/Irving Music Inc.
Revived by Chad Mitchell (Silver City, 91) and Suzy Bogguss on *Aces* (Capitol, 91).

**Over the Brooklyn Bridge**
Music by Marvin Hamlisch, words by Alan Bergman and Marilyn Bergman.
Threesome Music, 1991/Polygram Music Publishing Inc./Famous Music Corp.
Introduced by Art Garfunkel as the theme for the TV series *Brooklyn Bridge*.

# P

**Part of You, Part of Me**
Words and music by Glenn Frey and Jack Tempchin.
Jazz Bird Music, 1991/Red Cloud Music Co./Night River Publishing.
Introduced by Glenn Frey in the film and on the soundtrack album
  *Thelma & Louise* (MCA, 91).

**P.A.S.S.I.O.N.**
Words and music by Carl Sturken and Evan Rogers.
Bayjun Beat, 1991.
Best-selling record by Rythm Syndicate on *Rythm Syndicate* (Impact,
  91). This year's premiere dance mavens.

**Payin' the Cost to Be the Boss**
Words and music by B. B. King.
Duchess Music Corp., 1968/Sounds of Lucille Inc.
Revived by Pat Benatar on *True Love* (Chrysalis, 91). Former thrush
  attempts to sing the blues.

**People Are Still Having Sex**
Words and music by La Tour.
Take 2, 1991.
Best-selling record by La Tour from *La Tour* (Smash, 91).

**Perfect World**
Words and music by Glen Burtnik and Steve Krikorian.
Hampstead Heath Music Publishers Ltd., 1991/WB Music
  Corp./Polygram Songs/Polygram International.
Introduced by Alias in the film and on the soundtrack album *Don't
  Tell Mom the Babysitter's Dead* (Giant, 91).

**Phone Call from Leavenworth**
Words and music by Chris Whitley.
Reata Publishing Inc., 1991/Siete Leguas Music.
Introduced by Chris Whitley on *Living with the Law* (Columbia, 91).

### Piece of My Heart
Words and music by Tara Kemp, Jake Smith, and Tuhin Roy.
Kallman Music, Inc., 1991/One-Two.
Best-selling record by Michael W. Smith from *Go West Young Man* (Reunion, 91). Best-selling record by Tara Kemp from *Tara Kemp* (Giant, 91).

### Place in This World
Words and music by Wayne Kirkpatrick, Amy Grant, and Michael W. Smith.
Emily Boothe, 1991/Age to Age/O'Ryan Music, Inc.
Best-selling record by Michael W. Smith from *Go West Young Man* (Reunion, 91).

### Places That Belong to You
Words by Alan Bergman and Marilyn Bergman, music by James Newton Howard.
Burbank Plaza, 1991/Threesome Music/Emanuel Music/Aron Gate/Newton House Music/Music Corp. of America/Deco Music.
Introduced by Barbra Streisand on the soundtrack album *Prince of Tides* (Columbia, 91).

### Play That Funky Music
Words and music by Rob Parrissi, words by Vanilla Ice.
Ice Baby, 1976/QPM/EMI-Blackwood Music Inc./ICBD.
Best-selling record by Vanilla Ice from *To the Extreme* (SBK, 90).

### Play the Music for Me
Words and music by Jellyroll Morton, music by Luther Henderson, words by Susan Birkenhead.
Edwin H. Morris.
Performed by Tanya Pinkins in the musical *Jelly's Last Jam* (90) based on the works of Jellyroll Morton, due for Broadway in 1992.

### Playground
Words and music by Dallas Austin, Michael Bivins, and K. Wales.
Diva One, 1991/Mike Ten.
Best-selling record by Another Bad Creation from *Coolin' at the Playground Ya' Know* (Motown, 91).

### Point of Light
Words and music by Don Schlitz and Tom Schuyler.
Don Schlitz Music, 1991/EMI-Blackwood Music Inc./Bethlehem/Almo Music Corp.
Best-selling record by Randy Travis from *Heroes and Friends* (Warner Bros., 90). Making use of President Bush's campaign catch phrase.

**Poor Back Slider**
Words and music by Greg Brown.
Brown/Feldman, 1990.
Introduced by Greg Brown on *Down in There* (Red House, 90).

**Popskull**
Words and music by Curt Kirkwood.
Meat Puppets, 1991.
Introduced by Meat Puppets on *Forbidden Places* (London, 91).

**The Power Lines**
Words and music by Nanci Griffith and Pat Alger, music by James
    Hooker.
Irving Music Inc., 1991/Ponder Heart Music/Bait and Beer/Rick
    Hall Music.
Introduced by Nanci Griffith on *Late Night Grande Hotel* (MCA, 91).

**Power of Love/Love Power**
Words and music by Luther Vandross, Marcus Miller, and Teddy
    Vann (pseudonym for Theodore Williams).
EMI-April Music Inc., 1991/Uncle Ronnie's Music Co., Inc.,
    1991/Thriller Miller Music, 1991/MCA Music, 1991/Unbelievable,
    1967.
Best-selling record by Luther Vandross from *Power of Love* (Epic, 91).
    Medley in part with Sand Pebbles' 1967 hit "Love Power." Won a
    Grammy Award, Best Rhythm 'n' Blues Song of the Year .

**Pretzel Logic**
Words and music by Walter Becker and Donald Fagen.
MCA Music, 1974.
Revived by The New York Rock and Soul Revue on *Live at the Beacon*
    (Giant, 91). Marked Fagen's return to performing live.

**Prisoners of Their Hair**
Words and music by Christine Lavin.
Flip-a-Jig, 1990.
Introduced by Christine Lavin on *Fast Folk Musical Magazine* (Fast
    Folk, 91). Also included on *Compass* (Philo, 91).

**Private Line**
Words and music by Gerald Levert.
Trycep Publishing Co., 1991/Willesden Music, Inc.
Best-selling record by Gerald Levert from *Private Line* (East/West,
    91).

**The Promise of a New Day** (English)
Words and music by Peter Lord, Sondra St. Victor, V. Jeffrey Smith, and Paula Abdul.
EMI-April Music Inc., 1991/Leo Sun/Maanami/EMI-Blackwood Music Inc./Vernal.
Best-selling record by Paula Abdul from *Spellbound* (Capitol, 91).

**Psycho Street** (English)
Words and music by Richard Thompson.
Beeswing Music, 1991.
Introduced by Richard Thompson on *Rumor and Sigh* (Capitol, 91). Tour de force of controlled weirdness.

**Put Me in Your Mix**
Words and music by Barry White and Howard Johnson.
Seven Songs, 1991/Two Sioux.
Best-selling record by Barry White from *Put Me in Your Mix* (A & M, 91). A return of the master crooner.

# Q

**Quicksand Jesus**
Words and music by Rachel Bolan and Dave Sabo.
Wordiks, 1991/New Jersey Underground.
Introduced by Skid Row on *Slave to the Grind* (Atlantic, 91).

# R

**Rainbow Heart**
Words and music by Julia Fordham.
Island Music, 1991.
Introduced by Julia Fordham on *Swept* (Virgin, 91).

**Raised on Promises**
Words and music by Sam Phillips.
Eden Bridge Music, 1991.
Introduced by Sam Phillips on *Cruel Inventions* (Virgin, 91).

**Ray's Dad's Cadillac**
Words and music by Joni Mitchell.
Crazy Crow Music, 1991.
Introduced by Joni Mitchell on *Night Ride Home* (Geffen, 91).

**Read About Love** (English)
Words and music by Richard Thompson.
Beeswing Music, 1991.
Introduced by Richard Thompson on *Rumor and Sigh* (Capitol, 91).

**The Real Deal**
Words and music by Lifers' Group.
Introduced by Lifers' Group on *Lifers' Group* (Hollywood Basic, 91).
Words of warning from prison inmates. Made as part of the Lifers'
Group Juvenile Awareness program.

**Real Real Real** (English)
Words and music by Jesus Jones.
EMI Music Publishing, Ltd., London, England, 1990/EMI-
Blackwood Music Inc.
Best-selling record by Jesus Jones from *Doubt* (SBK, 91).
Breakthrough alternative/dance music for the rock crowd.

**Renegade**
Words and music by Warren Zevon.

Zevon Music Inc., 1991/Warner-Tamerlane Publishing Corp.
Introduced by Warren Zevon on *Mr. Bad Example* (Giant, 91).

### Rescue Me
Words and music by Madonna Ciccone and Shep Pettibone.
WB Music Corp., 1990/Bleu Disque Music/Webo Girl/Lexor.
Best-selling record by Madonna from *The Immaculate Collection* (Sire, 90).

### Restless
Words and music by Carl Perkins.
Cedarwood Publishing Co., Inc., 1969.
Revived by Mark O'Connor on *The New Nashville Cats* (Warner Bros., 91). O'Connor's band includes Steve Wariner, Ricky Skaggs, and Vince Gill.

### Resurrection
Words and music by Robbie Robertson.
Medicine Hat Music, 1991/EMI-April Music Inc.
Introduced by Robbie Robertson on *Storyville* (Geffen, 91).

### Rhythm of My Heart
Words and music by Marc Jordan and John Capek.
WB Music Corp., 1984/Jamm/Bibo Music Publishers.
Best-selling record by Gerardo from *Mo' Ritmo* (Interscope, 91). Best-selling record by Rod Stewart from *Vagabond Heart* (Warner Bros., 91).

### Rico Suave
Words and music by Gerardo (pseudonym for Gerardo Mejia) and Christian Carlos Warren.
Mo' Ritmo/Louis St.
Best-selling record by Gerardo from *Mo' Ritmo* (Interscope, 91).

### Ricochet
Words and music by Ice-T.
Rhyme Syndicate, 1901.
Introduced by Ice-T in the film and on the soundtrack of *Ricochet* (Sire, 91). Rap star in starring role.

### Right Down to It
Words and music by L. A. Reid (pseudonym for Antonio Reid), Babyface (pseudonym for Kenny Edmunds), and Daryl Simmons.
Kear Music, 1991/Sony Epic/Solar/Green Skirt Music.
Best-selling record by Damian Dane from *Damian Dane* (Laface, 91).

### Right Here, Right Now (English)
Words and music by Mike Edwards.

EMI-Blackwood Music Inc., 1990.
Best-selling record by Jesus Jones frm *Doubt* (SBK, 91). Commentary on events in Eastern Europe, with a dance/rock/alternative groove.

**Ring My Bell**
Words and music by Frederick Knight.
Two Knight Publishing Co., 1978.
Best-selling record by D.J. Jazzy Jeff & The Fresh Prince from *Homebase* (Jive, 91).

**Rite of Spring**
Words and music by Willie Nile.
Watercolor Music, 1991.
Introduced by Willie Nile on *Places I Have Never Been* (Columbia, 91).

**Rocket Man** (English)
Music by Elton John, words by Bernie Taupin.
Dick James Music Inc., 1972.
Revived by Kate Bush on *Two Rooms: Celebrating the Songs of Elton John and Berni Taupin* (Polydor, 91).

**Rocket o' Love**
Words and music by Doug Fieger and Burton Averre.
Zen Cruisers Music, 1990.
Introduced by The Knack on *Serious Fun* (Charisma, 91). Comeback efforts of unlamented power pop posers after nearly a decade.

**Rockin' Around the Christmas Tree**
Words and music by Johnny Marks.
St. Nicholas Music, Inc., 1960.
Revived by Brenda Lee on *A Brenda Lee Christmas* (Warner Bros., 91).

**Rockin' Years**
Words and music by Gary Smith and Frieda Parton.
Southern Gallery, 1990.
Best-selling record by Dolly Parton with Ricky Van Shelton on *Backroads* (Columbia, 90).

**Rodeo**
Words and music by Larry Bastian.
Rio Bravo, 1991.
Best-selling record by Garth Brooks from *Ropin' the Wind* (Capitol, 91).

**Roll the Bones** (Canadian)
Words and music by Geddy Lee and Alex Lifeson, words by Neil Peart.

Core Music Publishing, 1991.
Introduced by Rush on *Roll the Bones* (Atlantic, 91).

### Romantic
Words and music by Karyn White, Jimmy Jam (pseudonym for
James Harris, III), and Terry Lewis.
Warner-Tamerlane Publishing Corp., 1991/Kings Kid/Flyte Tyme
Tunes.
Best-selling record by Karyn White from *Ritual of Love* (Warner Bros.,
91).

### Round and Round
Words and music by Prince Rogers Nelson.
Controversy Music, 1990/WB Music Corp.
Best-selling record by Tevin Campbell from *Graffiti Bridge* (Paisley
Park, 90).

### Rumor Has It
Words and music by Bruce Burch, Vern Dant, and Larry Shell.
Ensign Music Corp., 1990/Sheddhouse Music/Millhouse.
Best-selling record by Reba McEntire from *Rumor Has It* (MCA, 90).

### Running Back to You
Words and music by Kenni Hairston and Trevor Gale.
Hiss N' Tell, 1991/Gale Warnings.
Best-selling record by Vanessa Williams from *The Comfort Zone*
(Wing/Mercury, 91).

### Rush Rush (English)
Words and music by Philip Lord.
EMI-April Music Inc., 1991/Leo Sun.
Best-selling record by Paula Abdul from *Spellbound* (Captive, 91).

### Rusted Pipe
Words and music by Suzanne Vega and Anton Sanko.
Waifersongs Ltd., 1990/Red Rubber/WB Music Corp.
Revived by DNA featuring Suzanne Vega on *Tom's Album* (A & M,
91). Introduced by Suzanne Vega on *Days of Open Hand* (A & M,
90). Another rap remix of the popular song poet.

# S

**Sadeness, Part 1** (East German)
Words and music by M. C. Curly, F. Gregorian, and David Fairstein.
Sweet n' Sour, 1991/Virgin Music, Inc.
Best-selling record by Enigma from *MCMXC A.D.* (Charisma, 91).

**Sam**
Words and music by Curt Kirkwood.
Meat Puppets, 1991.
Introduced by Meat Puppets on *Forbidden Places* (London, 91).
  Veteran alternative rockers back in form.

**Save Some Love**
Words and music by Greg Gerard.
Geffen Again Music, 1991/Gerard Video/Warner-Tamerlane
  Publishing Corp.
Best-selling record by Keedy from *Chase the Clouds* (Arista, 91).

**Searchin' for a Heart**
Words and music by Warren Zevon.
Donna Dijon Music, 1990/Zevon Music Inc.
Performed by Warren Zevon in the film *Grand Canyon* (91). Also on
  his album *Mr. Bad Example* (Giant, 91). Introduced in 1990 in the
  film *Love at Large*.

**Sensitivity**
Words and music by James Harris, III and Terry Lewis.
Flyte Tyme Tunes, 1989.
Best-selling record by Ralph Tresvant from *Ralph Tresvant* (MCA, 90).

**Series of Dreams**
Words and music by Bob Dylan.

Special Rider Music, 1989.
Introduced by Bob Dylan on *The Bootleg Series, Volumes 1-3 (Rare and Unreleased) 1961-1991* (Columbia, 91). New release from collection of vintage Dylan.

**Set Adrift on Memory Bliss** (English)
Words and music by Attrell Cordes and Gary Kemp.
MCA Music, 1991/Reformation Publishing USA.
Best-selling record by P.M. Dawn from *Of the Heart, of the Soul and of the Cross* (Gee Street/Island, 91).

**Set Me in Motion**
Words and music by Bruce Hornsby and John Hornsby.
Zappo Music, 1991/Basically Gasp Music/Bob-a-Lew Songs.
Introduced by Bruce Hornsby and the Range in the film and on the soundtrack *Backdraft* (RCA, 91).

**Set the Night to Music**
Words and music by Diane Warren.
Realsongs, 1990.
Best-selling record by Roberta Flack and Maxi Priest from *Set the Night to Music* (Atlantic, 91).

**Sexuality** (English)
Words and music by Billy Bragg and Johnny Marr.
Utilitarian Music (England), 1991/Marrs Songs Ltd./Warner-Tamerlane Publishing Corp.
Introduced by Billy Bragg on *Don't Try This at Home* (Elektra, 91). New area of interest for noted political performer.

**Shameless**
Words and music by Billy Joel.
Joelsongs, 1990.
Revived by Garth Brooks on *Ropin' the Wind* (Capitol, 91). The country performer takes on a pop tune.

**She Broke My Heart (in 36 Places)** (English)
Words and music by Londonbeat.
Warner-Tamerlane Publishing Corp., 1991.
Introduced by Londonbeat on *In the Blood* (Radioactive, 91).

**She Talks to Angels**
Words and music by Rich Robinson and Chris Robinson.
Enough to Contend With, 1990/Def USA.
Best-selling record by The Black Crowes from *Shake Your Moneymaker* (Def American, 90).

**She's in Love with the Boy**
Words and music by John Ims.
Warner-Elektra-Asylum Music Inc., 1991/Rites of Passage.
Best-selling record by Trisha Yearwood from *Trisha Yearwood* (MCA, 91).

**She's Just Dancing**
Words and music by David Wilcox.
Irving Music Inc., 1991/Midnight Ocean Bonfire.
Introduced by David Wilcox on *Home Again* (A & M, 91). Reviving the fine act of the singer/songwriter.

**Shiny Happy People**
Words and music by Peter Buck, William Berry, Mike Mills, and Michael Stipe.
Night Garden Music, 1991/Unichappell Music Inc.
Best-selling record by REM on *Out of Time* (Warner Bros., 91).

**Shot of Poison**
Words and music by Lita Ford, Jim Vallance, and Myron Grumbacher.
EMI-April Music Inc., 1991/Lisabella Music/Almo Music Corp./Testatyme/Tyreach.
Introduced by Lita Ford on *Dangerous Curves* (RCA, 91).

**Show Me the Way**
Words and music by Dennis DeYoung.
Grand Illusion Music, 1990/Almo Music Corp.
Best-selling record by Styx from *Edge of the Century* (A & M, 90). Adopted by U.S. as a patriotic theme for Operation Desert Storm.

**Signs**
Words and music by Les Emmerson.
Acuff-Rose Publications Inc., 1970/Galeneye.
Revived by Tesla from *Five Man Acoustical Jam* (Geffen, 90).

**Silent Lucidity**
Words and music by Chris DeGarmo.
Screen Gems-EMI Music Inc., 1991/Tri Ryche.
Best-selling record by Queensryche from *Empire* (EMI, 91). In the mold of Pink Floyd, a classic rock smash. Nominated for a Grammy Award, Best Rock Song of the Year .

**Sing Your Life** (English)
Words and music by Morrissey and Mark Nevin.
Bona Relations Music, 1991/Warner-Tamerlane Publishing Corp.
Introduced by Morrissey on *Kill Uncle* (Sire/Reprise, 91).

**'64 Ford**
Words and music by Phranc.
Folkswim, 1991.
Introduced by Phranc on *Positively Phranc* (Island, 91).

**The Small Glance** (English)
Words by Amy Powers, music by Andrew Lloyd Webber.
Really Useful Group, 1991.
Introduced by Elaine Paige on a TV show *An Evening with David Frost* (91). From the forthcoming musical, *Sunset Boulevard*.

**Small Town Saturday Night**
Words and music by Pat Alger and Hank Devito.
Bait and Beer, 1991/Forerunner/Little Nemo/Bug Music.
Best-selling record by Hal Ketchum from *Past the Point of Rescue* (Curb, 91).

**Smells Like Teen Spirit**
Words by Kurt Cobain, music by Nirvana.
Virgin Songs, 1991/End of Music.
Best-selling record by Nirvana on *Nevermind* (DGC, 91). Seattle-based band's alternative song of the year, written in reaction to the popular feminine deodorant.

**So Like Candy** (English)
Words and music by Declan MacManus and Paul McCartney.
Plangent Visions Music, Inc., London, England/MPL
    Communications Inc., 1991.
Introduced by Elvis Costello on *Mighty Like a Rose* (Warner Bros., 91).

**So Many Millions**
Words and music by John Norwood Fisher and Angelo Moore.
Music Corp. of America, 1991/Bouillabaisse Music.
Introduced by Fishbone on *The Reality of My Surroundings* (Columbia, 91).

**So Much Love**
Words and music by Felton Pilate.
Bust It Publishing.
Best-selling record by B Angie B from *B Angie B* (Bust It/Capitol, 91).

**Soapbox Preacher**
Words and music by Robbie Robertson.
Medicine Hat Music, 1991/EMI-April Music Inc.
Introduced by Robbie Robertson on *Storyville* (Geffen, 91).

**Someday**
Words and music by Mariah Carey and Ben Marguiles.
Vision of Love Songs Inc., 1989/Been Jammin' Music.
Best-selling record by Mariah Carey from *Mariah Carey* (Columbia, 90).

**Someday**
Words and music by Alan Jackson and Jim McBride.
Mattie Ruth, 1991/Seventh Son Music Inc./EMI-April Music Inc.
Best-selling record by Alan Jackson from *Don't Rock the Jukebox* (Arista, 91).

**Someday Soon**
Words and music by Ian Tyson.
WB Music Corp., 1963.
Revived by Suzy Bogguss on *Aces* (Capitol, 91).

**Someone to Love**
Words and music by Roger McGuinn and Camilla McGuinn.
McGuinn Music, 1990/April First.
Introduced by Roger McGuinn on *Back from Rio* (Arista, 90).

**Something Else to Me**
Words and music by Jules Shear.
Juters Publishing Co./Music Corp. of America.
Introduced by Jules Shear on *The Great Puzzle* (Polydor, 91).
    Regarded as one of rock's quality quirky songwriters.

**Something in My Heart**
Words and music by Michel'le and Dr Dre (pseudonym for Andre
    Young).
Ruthless Attack Muzick, 1990.
Best-selling record by Miche'le from *Michel'le* (Ruthless/Atlantic, 90).

**Something to Believe In**
Words and music by Bobby Dall, C. C. DeVille, Bret Michaels, and
    Rikki Rockett.
Cyanide, 1990/Willesden Music, Inc.
Best-selling record by Poison from *Flesh and Blood* (Enigma, 90).

**Something to Talk About** (Canadian)
Words and music by Shirley Eikhard.
Convee, 1991/Lynn Jacobs Publishing.
Best-selling record by Bonnie Raitt from *Luck of the Draw* (Capitol, 91). Nominated for a Grammy Award, Best Song of the Year.

**Somewhere in My Broken Heart**
Words and music by Billy Dean and Rich Leigh.
EMI-Blackwood Music Inc., 1991/EMI-April Music Inc./Lion
    Hearted Music.
Best-selling record by Billy Dean from *Young Man* (SBK, 91).

**Somewhere in My Memory (from *Home Alone*)**
Words by Leslie Bricusse, music by John Williams.
Fox Film Music Corp., 1990.
Introduced by The Boston Pops Orchestra and Choir, conducted by
    John Williams in the film *Home Alone* (90). Nominated for a
    Grammy Award, Best Song Written for a Film.

**Song of Baltimore**
Words and music by Jane Gillman.
Red Linnet, 1990/Pterodactyl.
Introduced by Jane Gillman on *Jane Gillman* (Green Linnet, 91).

**The Soul Cages**
Words and music by Sting.
Magnetic, England, 1991/Blue Turtle.
Introduced by Sting on *The Soul Cages* (A & M, 91). Won a Grammy
    Award, Best Rock Song of the Year .

**Special**
Words and music by Vesta Williams and Attala Zane Giles.
Vesta Seven, 1991/Almo Music Corp./Captain Z.
Best-selling record by Vesta from *Special* (A & M, 91).

**Stand by Me**
Words and music by Jerry Leiber, Mike Stoller, and Ben E. King.
Jerry Leiber Music, 1961/Mike Stoller Music/Unichappell Music Inc.
Revived by Ben E. King on *There's a Riot Goin' On: The Rock 'n' Roll
    Classics of Leiber & Stoller* (Rhino, 91). Vintage tracks from
    pioneering songwriters of early rock and Rhythm 'n' Blues .

**The Star Spangled Banner**
Words and music by Francis Scott Key.
Public Domain.
Best-selling record by Whitney Houston (Arista, 91). As heard during
    the Super Bowl and released to capitalize on patriotic feelings early
    in the year.

**Steel Rails**
Words and music by Louise Branscomb.

One Note Publishing, 1990/Sawgrass Music.
Introduced by Alison Krauss on *I've Got That Old Feeling* (Rounder, 90). Bluegrass breakthrough of the year.

**Stepping Out**
Words by Fred Ebb, music by John Kander.
Fiddleback Music Publishing Co., Inc., 1991.
Introduced by Liza Minnelli at a benefit performance for the Drama League.

**Stone Cold Gentleman**
Words and music by Daryl Simmons, Kayo, L. A. Reid (pseudonym for Antonio Reid), Louis Johnson, Bobby Brown, and Ralph Tresvant.
Kear Music, 1990/Solar/Green Skirt Music/Sony Epic/MCA Music.
Best-selling record by Ralph Tresvant from *Ralph Tresvant* (MCA, 90).

**Street of Dreams**
Words and music by Carl Sturken and Evan Rogers.
Warner-Tamerlane Publishing Corp., 1991/Could Be Music/Bayjun Beat.
Best-selling record by Nia Peeples from *Nia Peeples* (Charisma, 91).

**Strike It Up** (Italian)
Words and music by Mirko Limoni, Daniele Davoli, and Valerio Semplici.
Lambardoni Edizioni, 1990/Intersong, USA Inc.
Best-selling record by Black Box from *Dreemland* (RCA, 90).

**Summer Nights**
Music by Charles Strouse, words by Stephen Schwartz.
Charles Strouse Music, 1986/Grey Dog Music.
Revived in *Rap* (91).

**Summertime**
Words and music by A. Taylor, Robert Mickens, Robert Bell, George Brown, Richard Westerfield, Dennis Thomas, Clydes Smith, Ronald Bell, K. Hula, Fingers, and Will Smith.
Warner-Tamerlane Publishing Corp., 1991/Second Decade Music/Da Posse's/Willesden Music, Inc./Zomba Enterprises, Inc.
Best-selling record by D. J. Jazzy Jeff & The Fresh Prince from *Homebase* (Jive, 91).

**Sunless Saturday**
Words and music by Kendall Jones.
Bouillabaisse Music, 1991/Music Corp. of America.
Introduced by Fishbone on *The Reality of My Surroundings* (Columbia, 91). Steaming hunk of rock/funk.

**Surrender**
Words and music by Rick Nielsen.
Screen Gems-EMI Music Inc., 1976.
Revived by Cheap Trick on *The Greatest Hits* (Epic, 91).

# T

**Take a Giant Step**
Words by Gerry Goffin, music by Carole King.
Screen Gems-EMI Music Inc., 1966.
Performed by Taj Mahal on *Like Never Before* (Private Music, 91).

**Take a Look at My Heart**
Words and music by John Prine.
Bruised Oranges, 1990.
Introduced by John Prine on *The Missing Years* (Oh Boy, 91).

**Take This Longing** (Canadian)
Words and music by Leonard Cohen.
Stranger Music Inc., 1974.
Revived by Peter Astor on *I'm Your Fan: The Songs of Leonard Cohen*
  (Atlantic, 91). Eclectic reading of one of the poet's greatest works.

**Tame Yourself**
Words and music by Myoshin Thurman, Michael Kolasa, and Flair
  Smithjones.
Juicy, 1991.
Introduced by Raw Youth on *Tame Yourself* (Rhino, 91). Reacting in
  favor of animal rights.

**Tears in Heaven** (English)
Words and music by Eric Clapton and Will Jennings.
Drumlin Ltd. (England), 1991.
Introduced by Eric Clapton in the film and on the soundtrack album
  *Rush* (Reprise, 91). Written for Clapton's late son, who died earlier
  in the year in a fall.

**Temptation**
Words and music by Corina, Franc Reyes, Carlos Berrios, and Luis
  Capri Duprey.

Corina Starr Music, 1991/King Reyes/Berrios/Cutting Music.
Best-selling record by Corina from *Corina* (Atco, 91).

**Tender Kisses**
Words and music by Matt Sherrod, Paul Sherrod, Sir Spence, and
    Tracie Spencer.
Zodroq, 1990/Zodboy/Sir Spence/Love Tone/M&T Spencer.
Best-selling record by Tracie Spencer from *Make the Difference*
    (Capitol, 90).

**Texarkana**
Words and music by Peter Buck, William Berry, Mike Mills, and
    Michael Stipe.
Night Garden Music, 1991/Unichappell Music Inc.
Introduced by REM on *Out of Time* (Warner Bros., 91).

**Thank You World** (English)
Words and music by Karl Wallinger.
Lew-Bob Songs, 1990/Polygram International.
Revived by World Party on *Thank You World* (Chrysalis, 91).

**That's Enough for Me**
Words and music by Willie Nile.
Watercolor Music, 1991.
Introduced by Willie Nile on *Places I Have Never Been* (Columbia, 91).

**That's What Love Is For**
Words and music by Michael Omartian, Mark Muller, and Amy
    Grant.
All Nations Music, 1991/Moo Maison/MCA Music/Age to
    Age/Reunion.
Best-selling record by Amy Grant from *Heart in Motion* (A & M, 91).

**Things That Make You Go Hmmm**
Words and music by Rob Clivilles and Freedom Williams.
Virgin Music, Inc., 1991/Cole-Clivilles/RGB-Dome.
Best-selling record by C & C Music Factory featuring Freedom
    Williams from *Gonna Make You Sweat* (Columbia, 91).

**This House**
Words and music by Matt Sherrod, Paul Sherrod, and Sir Spence.
Zodroq, 1990/Zodboy/Editions EG/Sir Spence/M&T Spencer.
Best-selling record by Tracie Spencer from *Make the Difference*
    (Capitol, 90).

**3 A.M. Eternal** (English)
Words and music by Jimi Cauty, Bill Drummond, and T. Thorpe.

Brampton Music Ltd., England/E.G. Music, Inc., 1991/Warner-Chappell Music/WB Music Corp.
Best-selling record by The KLF from *The White Room* (Arista, 91). Harbingers of new dance/rock blend.

### The Thunder Rolls
Words and music by Pat Alger and Garth Brooks.
Bait and Beer, 1988/Forerunner/Major Bob Music.
Best-selling record by Garth Brooks from *No Fences* (Capitol, 90). Attracted controversy for depiction of wife battering.

### Tie a Yellow Ribbon 'Round the Old Oak Tree
Words and music by Irvin Levine and L. Russell Brown.
Levine & Brown Music Inc., 1972.
Revived by Sonny James and Karla Taylor (Curb, 91). Revived to coincide with returning soldiers.

### Time after Time
Words and music by Cyndie Lauper and Rob Hyman.
Reilla Music Corp., 1983/Dub Notes/WB Music Corp.
Revived by Richie Havens on *Now* (Epic, 91).

### Time, Love and Tenderness
Words and music by Diane Warren.
Realsongs, 1991.
Best-selling record by Michael Bolton from *Time, Love and Tenderness* (Columbia, 91).

### Time Run Like a Freight Train
Words and music by Eric Andersen.
Wind and Sand Music, 1973.
Revived by Eric Andersen on *Stages: The Lost Album* (Columbia, 91). Long lost tapes of the stalwart folk/rocker.

### To My Donna
Words and music by Hank Shocklee, Keith Shocklee, Carl Ryder, Gary G. Wiz, Kamron, G. Standon, Firstborn, and Skribble.
Def American Songs, 1991.
Introduced by Young Black Teenagers on *Young Black Teenages* (Soul, 91). Using the groove for Public Enemy's "Security of the First World," on which Madonna's "Justify My Love" was based. Song is a takeoff on the diva.

### Tom's Diner
Words by Suzanne Vega.
AGF Music Ltd., 1987/Waifersongs Ltd.
Revived by DNA, with Suzanne Vega from *Jam Harder* (A & M, 90). Originally on Vega's *Solitude Standing* (A & M, 87).

**Too Many Walls** (English)
Words and music by Cathy Dennis and Anne Dudley.
Colgems-EMI Music Inc., 1991/Buffalo/EMI-April Music Inc.
Best-selling record by Cathy Dennis from *Move to This* (Polydor, 91).

**Top of the Pops**
Words and music by Pat DiNizio.
Screen Gems-EMI Music Inc., 1991/Famous Monsters Music.
Introduced by The Smithereens on *Blow Up* (Capitol, 91).

**Touch Me (All Night Long)** (English)
Words and music by Delyle Carmichael and Patrick Adams.
Larry Spier, Inc., 1991/Personal Music.
Best-selling record by Cathy Dennis from *Move to This* (Polydor, 91).

**Toy Balloon**
Words and music by George Fischoff.
Screen Gems-EMI Music Inc., 1970.
Introduced in *Georgie Girl* revival, it was not included in original
   production.

**Truckin'**
Words and music by Robert Hunter, Jerry Garcia, Bob Weir, and
   Phil Lesh.
Ice Nine Publishing Co., Inc., 1971.
Revived by Dwight Yoakam on *Deadicated* (Arista, 91). Interpreting
   The Grateful Dead classic.

**2 Legit to Quit**
Words and music by Hammer, Felton Pilate, James Earley, Michael
   Kelly, and Louis Burrell.
Bust It Publishing, 1991.
Best-selling record by Hammer from *Too Legit to Quit* (Capitol, 91).

**Two Medicines**
Words and music by Pat MacDonald and Barbara K. MacDonald.
Mambadaddi, 1990/I.R.S.
Introduced by Timbuk 3 on *Big Shot in the Dark* (I.R.S., 91).

**Two Minute Brother**
Words and music by Mark Sexx and Lyndah.
Introduced by BWP on *The Bytches* (No Face, 91).

**Two of a Kind, Workin' on a Full House**
Words and music by Bobby Boyd, Warren Haynes, and Dennis
   Robbins.
Muhlenberg: World Wide Music, Inc., 1987/Cal Cody/Wee B Music.
Best-selling record by Garth Brooks from *Influences* (Capitol, 90).

# U

**Unbelievable** (English)
Words and music by James Atkin, Ian Dench, Zak Foley, Mark
   Decloedt, and Derry Brownson.
WB Music Corp.
Best-selling record by EMF from *Schubert Dip* (EMI, 91).

**Unforgettable**
Words and music by Irving Gordon.
Bourne Co., 1951.
Revived by Natalie Cole with Nat 'King' Cole on *Unforgettable*
   (Elektra, 91). Through the magic of technology, a long awaited duet.
   Won Grammy Awards, Best Song of the Year and Best Record of
   the Year.

**Used to Be**
Words and music by Patty Larkin.
Lamartine, 1991/Lost Lake Arts Music.
Introduced by Patty Larkin on *Tango* (High Street, 91). A new voice in
   folk/rock.

# V

**Valentine**
Words and music by Nils Lofgren.
Hilmer Music Publishing Co., 1990.
Introduced by Nils Lofgren on *Silver Lining* (Ryko, 91).

**The Very Thing**
Words and music by Sara Hickman and Sandy Abernathy.
Esta Chica, 1990/Music Corp. of America.
Introduced by Sara Hickman on *Shortstop* (Elektra, 90).

**Voices That Care**
Words and music by David Foster, Peter Cetera, and Linda
  Thompson Jenner.
Air Bear, 1990/Linda's Boys Music/Warner-Tamerlane Publishing
  Corp./Fall Line Orange Music.
Best-selling record by Voices That Care (Giant, 91). Patriotic
  sentiments purveyed by an all-star cast.

# W

**Waiting for Love** (Canadian)
Words and music by Brett Walker and Geoffrey Leib.
Walker Avenue, 1991/Leibraphone/Polygram Songs/Songs of
   Polygram.
Best-selling record by Alias from *Alias* (EMI, 91).

**The Walk**
Words and music by Mark Miller.
Zoo II Music, 1991.
Best-selling record by Sawyer Brown from *Buick* (Curb/Capitol, 91).

**Walk on Faith**
Words and music by Mike Reed and Allen Shamblin.
Almo Music Corp., 1990/Brio Blues/Hayes Street.
Best-selling record by Mike Reid from *Turning for Home* (Columbia,
   90).

**Walkin' Around**
Words and music by Marshall Crenshaw.
Belwin-Mills Publishing Corp., 1991/MHC Music.
Introduced by Marshall Crenshaw on *Life's Too Short* (Paradox/MCA,
   91).

**Walking Down Madison**
Words and music by Kirsty MacColl and Johnny Marr.
Virgin Songs, 1991/Warner-Tamerlane Publishing Corp./Warner-
   Chappell Music.
Introduced by Kirsty MacColl from *Electric Landlady* (Charisma, 91).

**Walking in Memphis**
Words and music by Marc Cohn.

Museum Steps Music, 1991.
Best-selling record by Marc Cohn from *Marc Cohn* (Atlantic, 91).
   Nominated for a Grammy Award, Best Song of the Year.


### Wanted Man
Words and music by Bob Dylan and Johnny Cash.
Big Sky Music, 1969.
Revived by Johnny Cash (Mercury, 91).

### War Song
Words and music by Vinnie James.
BMG Music, 1991.
Introduced by Vinnie James on *All American Boy* (RCA, 91).

### The Way You Do the Things You Do
Words and music by William "Smokey" Robinson and Ronnie
   Rodgers.
Jobete Music Co., Inc., 1964.
Revived by UB40 on *Labour of Love II* (Virgin, 90).

### We Both Walk
Words and music by Tom Shapiro and Chris Waters.
Edge o' the Woods, 1991/Kinetic Diamond/Moline Valley.
Best-selling record by Lorrie Morgan from *Something in Red* (RCA,
   91).

### We Don't Wanna Grow Up
Words by Leslie Bricusse, music by John Williams.
Triple Star/Marjer Publishing/Stage & Screen Music Inc.
Introduced by Children's Chorus in the movie and on the soundtrack
   of *Hook* (Epic, 91).

### We Want the Funk
Words and music by Gerardo (pseudonym for Gerardo Mejia),
   George Clinton, Jr., Bootsy Collins, and Jerome Brailey.
Mo' Ritmo, 1976/EMI-April Music Inc./Bridgeport Music Inc.
Best-selling record by Gerardo from *Mo' Ritmo* (Interscope, 91). Based
   on the Funkadelic hit "Tear the Roof Off the Sucker."

### Wham
Music by Lonnie Mack.
Trio Music Co., Inc., 1963/Fort Knox Music Co.
Revived by Stevie Ray Vaughan and Double Trouble on *The Sky Is
   Crying* (Epic, 91). Mack was one of the late blues guitarist's early
   idols.

**What Comes Naturally**
Words and music by Antonia Armato and Nick Mundy.
Tom Sturges, 1991/Chrysalis Music Corp./Warner-Tamerlane
  Publishing Corp./Nick Mundy/GG Loves Music.
Best-selling record by Sheena Easton from *What Comes Naturally*
  (MCA, 91).

**Whatever You Want**
Words and music by Dwayne Wiggins and Caron Wheeler.
Tony! Toni! Tone!, 1990/PRI Music.
Best-selling record by Tony! Toni! Tone! from *The Revival* (Wing, 90).

**When a Man Loves a Women**
Words and music by Calvin Lewis and Andrew Wright.
Pronto Music, Inc., 1966/Quinvy Music Publishing Co./Warner-
  Tamerlane Publishing Corp.
Revived by Michael Bolton on *Time, Love and Tenderness* (Columbia,
  91).

**When It Began**
Words and music by Paul Westerberg.
NAH Music, 1990.
Released by The Replacements on *All Shook Down* (Sire, 91). Also
  found on promotional release *Don't Sell or Buy, It's Crap.*

**When the Night Comes Down** (Scottish)
Words and music by Jimmie O'Neill.
Copyright Control, 1991.
Introduced by The Silencers on *Dance to the Holy Man* (BMG, 91).

**When You're Alone**
Words by Leslie Bricusse, music by John Williams.
Triple Star/Marjer Publishing/Stage & Screen Music Inc.
Introduced by Amber Scott in the film and on the soundtrack LP *Hook*
  (Epic, 91).

**Where Are You Now**
Words and music by Clint Black and Hayden Nicholas.
Howlin' Hits Music, 1990.
Best-selling record by Clint Black from *Put Yourself in My Shoe* (RCA,
  90).

**Where Does My Heart Beat Now** (Canadian)
Words and music by Robert White Johnson and Taylor Rhodes.
Hit List, 1990/Dejamus California/Taylor Rhodes Music.
Best-selling record by Celine Dion from *Unison* (Epic, 91).

**Where the Colors Don't Go**
Words and music by Sam Phillips.
Eden Bridge Music, 1991.
Introduced by Sam Phillips on *Cruel Inventions* (Virgin, 91).

**Why Was I Born (Freddy's Dead)**
Words and music by Iggy Pop and Kirst.
Thousand Mile Inc., 1991/Christ & Co./Bug Music.
Introduced by Iggy Pop in the film and on the soundtrack *Freddy's Dead: The Final Nightmare* (Metal Blade, 91).

**Wicked Game**
Words and music by Chris Isaak.
Chris Isaak Music Publishing, 1990.
Best-selling record by Chris Isaak from *Heart-Shaped World* (Reprise, 90).

**Wild Night**
Words and music by Van Morrison.
WB Music Corp., 1971/Caledonia Productions.
Revived by Martha Reeves in the film and on the soundtrack album *Thelma & Louise* (MCA, 91).

**Wildside**
Words and music by Lou Reed, Spice, Donnie Wahlberg, and Mark Wahlberg.
Oakfield Avenue Music Ltd., 1972/Screen Gems-EMI Music Inc.
Best-selling record by Marky Mark & The Funky Bunch from *Music for the People* (Interscope, 91). Based on the Lou Reed classic "Walk on the Wild Side."

**Wind of Change** (East German)
Words and music by Klaus Meine.
Copyright Control, 1990.
Best-selling record by The Scorpions from *Crazy World* (Mercury, 90). Celebrating freedom in Eastern Europe.

**With You**
Words and music by Raymond Reeder.
Re-Deer, 1991/Sun Face Music Inc.
Best-selling record by Tony Terry from *Tony Terry* (Epic, 91).

**Woman in the Waves**
Words and music by Michael Franks.
Mississippi Mud, 1991/Warner-Tamerlane Publishing Corp.
Introduced by Michael Franks on *Blue Pacific* (Reprise, 91).

**Woman She Was Gentle**
Words and music by Eric Andersen.
Wind and Sand Music, 1973.
Revived by Eric Andersen on *Stages: The Lost Album* (Columbia, 91).

**Women with the Strength of 10,000 Men**
Words and music by Peter Himmelman.
Geffen Music, 1991/Himmasongs/WB Music Corp.
Introduced by Peter Himmelman on *From Strength to Strength* (Epic, 91).

**Word to the Badd**
Words and music by Babyface (pseudonym for Kenny Edmunds), Daryl Simmons, Jermaine Jackson, Lisa Lopes, and L. A. Reid (pseudonym for Antonio Reid).
Kear Music, 1991/Epic/Solar/Green Skirt Music/Black Stallion County Publishing/Pettibone.
Introduced by Jermaine Jackson on *You Said* (Laface, 91). A personal message from one Jackson to another.

**Working for the Japanese**
Words and music by Ronald Delacey.
Paul Craft, 1991.
Introduced by Ray Stevens (Curb/Capitol, 91). Astute commentary on today's financial state of affairs.

**Written All Over Your Face**
Words and music by Larry Marcus.
Trycep Publishing Co., 1990/Rude News.
Best-selling record by Rude Boys from *Rude Awakenings* (Atlantic, 90). The rap track of the year.

# Y

**Yakety Yak (Take It Back)**
Words and music by Jerry Leiber and Mike Stoller.
Jerry Leiber Music, 1958/Mike Stoller Music/Chappell & Co., Inc.
Updated by Queen Latifah, Stevie Wonder, Ozzy Osbourne, Tone Loc, Ricky Van Shelton, and Bette Midler (Atlantic, 91). Used as part of an awareness campaign for the Take It Back Foundation to promote recycling.

**You and the World**
Words by David Grover, music by Eddie Bydalek.
EMI-Blackwood Music Inc., 1991/Da Braddah's.
Introduced by Loud Sugar on *Loud Sugar* (SBK, 91).

**You Can't Play with My Yo Yo**
Words and music by Yo Yo, James Brown, Charles Sherall, and Ice Cube.
Gangsta Boogie, 1991/Street Knowledge/Dynatone/Unichappell Music Inc.
Introduced by Yo Yo, featuring Ice Cube on *Make Way for the Motherlode* (East-West, 91).

**You Can't Resist It**
Words and music by Lyle Lovett.
Michael H. Goldsen, Inc., 1991/Lyle Lovett.
Introduced by Lyle Lovett in the film and on the soundtrack *Switch* (MCA, 91). Nominated for a Grammy Award, Best Song Written for a Film.

**You Could Be Mine**
Words and music by Guns N' Roses.
Guns N' Roses Music, 1991.
Introduced by Guns N' Roses in the film and on the soundtrack to *Terminator 2: Judgement Day.*

**You Don't Have to Go Home Tonight**
Words and music by Eric Lowen, David Navarro, Diana Villegas, Sylvia Villegas, and Vicki Villegas.
Famous Music Corp., 1991/Careers-BMG/Sony Songs/Tres Hermanas/Salsongs/Marion Place.
Best-selling record by The Triplets in *Thicker Than Water* (Mercury, 91).

**You Don't Have to Worry**
Words and music by Thom McElroy and Denzil Foster.
Two Tuff-Enuff Publishing, 1990/Irving Music Inc.
Best-selling record by En Vogue from *Born to Sing* (Atlantic, 90).

**You Gotta Do What You Gotta Do**
Words and music by Erik Frandsen, Robert Hipkens, Michael Garin, and Paula Lockheart.
Introduced by Donna Murphy in *Song of Singapore* (91).

**You Know Me Better Than That**
Words and music by Tony Haselden and Anna Lisa Graham.
Millhouse, 1991/Sheddhouse Music.
Best-selling record by George Strait from *Chill of an Early Fall* (MCA, 91).

**Your Love Is a Miracle**
Words and music by Bill Kenner and Mark Wright.
Tom Collins Music Corp., 1990/EMI-Blackwood Music Inc./Wrightchild.
Best-selling record by Mark Chesnutt from *Too Cold at Home* (MCA, 90).

**Your One and Only**
Words and music by Even Stevens and Hilary Kanter.
Even Stevens, 1991/Hilary Kanter.
Introduced by Brenda Lee on *Brenda Lee* (Warner Bros., 91).

**You're in Love**
Words and music by Wilson Phillips, words and music by Glen Ballard.
EMI-Blackwood Music Inc., 1990/Wilphill/Braintree Music/MCA Music/Aerostation Corp.
Best-selling record by Wilson Phillips from *Wilson Phillips* (SBK, 90).

**Youth of 1,000 Summers**
Words and music by Van Morrison.
Van Morrison, 1991.
Introduced by Van Morrison on *Enlightenment* (Mercury, 91).

# Lyricists & Composers Index

# Lyricists & Composers Index

Baker, Jarvis La Rue
  I Love Your Smile
Ballard, Glen
  The Dream Is Still Alive
  You're in Love
Ballard, Greg
  I Wonder Why
Banks, Tony
  No Son of Mine
Barnes, Max T.
  Love Me
Barnes, Sharon
  Feels Like Another One
Bastian, Larry
  Rodeo
Becker, Walter
  Pretzel Logic
Belford, Pam
  If I Know Me
Bell, Robert
  Summertime
Bell, Ronald
  Summertime
Belle, Bernard
  I Like the Way (The Kissing Game)
  Let's Chill
Bergman, Alan
  Over the Brooklyn Bridge
  Places That Belong to You
Bergman, Marilyn
  Over the Brooklyn Bridge
  Places That Belong to You
Berrios, Carlos
  Temptation
Berry, Walter
  Losing My Religion
Berry, William
  Shiny Happy People
  Texarkana
Bettencourt, Nuno
  Hole Hearted
  More Than Words
Bettis, John
  Can You Stop the Rain?
Birkenhead, Susan
  Michigan Water
  Play the Music for Me

Bishop, Elvin
  Fooled Around and Fell in Love
Bivins, Michael
  Iesha
  Motownphilly
  Playground
Black, Clint
  Loving Blind
  Where Are You Now
Blackburn, Tom
  The Ballad of Davy Crockett
Blades, Jack
  High Enough
Bolan, Rachel
  Quicksand Jesus
Bolton, Michael
  Love Is a Wonderful Thing
Bon Jovi, Jon
  Miracle (from *Young Guns II*)
Bottrell, Bill
  Black or White
Bourke, Rory
  I Couldn't See You Leavin'
Bowles, Rick
  Down Home
Boyd, Bobby
  Two of a Kind, Workin' on a Full
    House
Brady, Paul
  Luck of the Draw
Bragg, Billy
  I Wish You Were Her
  Moving the Goalposts
  Sexuality
Brailey, Jerome
  We Want the Funk
Branscomb, Louise
  Steel Rails
Bricusse, Leslie
  Somewhere in My Memory (from
    *Home Alone*)
  We Don't Wanna Grow Up
  When You're Alone
Brooks, Garth
  The Thunder Rolls
Brooks, Kix
  Brand New Men
  My Next Broken Heart

Brooks, W. Allen
  Because I Love You (The Postman
    Song)
Brown, Bobby
  Stone Cold Gentleman
Brown, George
  Summertime
Brown, Greg
  Hillbilly Girl
  Poor Back Slider
Brown, James
  You Can't Play with My Yo-Yo
Brown, L. Russell
  Tie a Yellow Ribbon 'Round the Old
    Oak Tree
Brown, Stanley
  I'm Dreamin' (from *New Jack City*)
Brown, Vinnie
  Latifah's Had It Up to Here
  O.P.P.
Brownson, Derry
  Unbelievable
Bruns, George
  The Ballad of Davy Crockett
Buck, Peter
  Losing My Religion
  Shiny Happy People
  Texarkana
Burch, Bruce
  Rumor Has It
Burrell, Louis
  2 Legit to Quit
Burtnik, Glen
  Perfect World
Bydalek, Eddie
  You and the World
Byrne, David
  Once in a Lifetime
Cafferty, John
  On the Dark Side
Calderon, Jorge
  Mr. Bad Example
Capek, John
  Rhythm of My Heart
Carey, Mariah
  Can't Let Go
  Emotions
  I Don't Wanna Cry

If It's Over
Love Takes Time
Someday
Carmichael, Delyle
  Touch Me (All Night Long)
Carnelia, Craig
  The Kid Inside
  The Last 40 Years
Carpenter, Mary Chapin
  Down at the Twist and Shout
  Going Out Tonight
Carter, Carlene
  Come on Back
Cartwright, Lionel
  Leap of Faith
Cash, Johnny
  Wanted Man
Cauty, Jimi
  3 A.M. Eternal
Cetera, Peter
  Voices That Care
Chambers, Jimmy
  A Better Love
  I've Been Thinking About You
Chandler, George
  A Better Love
  I've Been Thinking About You
Chapman, Beth Neilsen
  Here We Are
Chapman, Percy Lee
  Arrest the President
Chaver, Ingrid
  Do Anything
Cherone, Gary
  Hole Hearted
  More Than Words
Child, Desmond
  The Gift of Life
  Obsession
Ciccone, Madonna
  Justify My Love
  Rescue Me
Clapton, Eric
  Tears in Heaven
Cleveland, Ashley
  Big Town
  I Could Learn to Love You

# Lyricists & Composers Index

# Lyricists & Composers Index

Himmelman, Peter
  Only Innocent
  Women with the Strength of 10,000
    Men
Hines, Gary
  Optimistic
Hipkens, Robert
  Never Pay Musicians What They're
    Worth
  You Gotta Do What You Gotta Do
Hodges, Warren
  Here I Am (Come and Take Me)
Holsapple, Peter
  Angels
Holyfield, Wayland
  Only Here for a Little While
Hooker, James
  The Power Lines
Horner, James
  Dream to Dream
Hornsby, Bruce
  Go Back to the Woods
  Set Me in Motion
Hornsby, John
  Set Me in Motion
Howard, James Newton
  Places That Belong to You
Howe, Brian
  If You Needed Somebody
Huff, Leon
  Now That We Found Love
Hula, K.
  Summertime
Hunter, Robert
  Bertha
  Truckin'
Hutchence, Mick
  Disappear
Hutchinson, Wanda
  I Don't Wanna Lose Your Love
Hyman, Rob
  Time after Time
Ice Cube
  You Can't Play with My Yo-Yo
Ice-T
  Ricochet

Ims, John
  Fallin' Out of Love
  She's in Love with the Boy
Isaak, Chris
  Don't Make Me Dream About You
  Wicked Game
Isbele, Alvertis
  I'll Take You There
Jackson, Alan
  Don't Rock the Jukebox
  Forever Together
  I'd Love You All Over Again
  Someday
Jackson, Bernard
  The First Time
Jackson, Brian
  Never Gonna Let You Down
Jackson, Jermaine
  Word to the Badd
Jackson, Joe
  Obvious Song
Jackson, Michael
  Black or White
Jackson, Sylvester
  I Love Your Smile
Jagger, Mick
  Highwire
Jam, Jimmy
  Optimistic
  Romantic
Jam, Sir
  I Wanna Be Like Mike
James, Rick
  Around the Way Girl
James, Vinnie
  War Song
Jane's Addiction
  Been Caught Stealing
Jarrard, John
  Mirror Mirror
Jarvis, John
  Love Can Build a Bridge
Jenkins, Marsha
  Kissing You
Jenner, Linda Thompson
  Voices That Care

# Lyricists & Composers Index

# Lyricists & Composers Index

Pop, Iggy
Why Was I Born (Freddy's Dead)
Popper, John
I Have My Moments
Powers, Amy
The Small Glance
Prestwood, Hugh
A Family Tie
Price, Reynolds
Copperline
Price, Terry
It Should've Been You
Prince & The New Power Generation
Cream
Gett Off
Prine, John
Let's Talk Dirty in Hawaiian
Take a Look at My Heart
Prof. T
Optimistic
Rabin, Trevor
Lift Me Up
Raitt, Bonnie
One Part Be My Lover
Ramones
I Wanna Be Your Boyfriend
Ramos, Duran
Let the Beat Hit 'Em
Reed, Lou
Wildside
Reed, Mike
Walk on Faith
Reeder, Raymond
With You
Reid, Antonio, see Reid, L. A.
Reid, L. A.
Exclusivity
Heat of the Moment
I'm Your Baby Tonight
Love Makes Things Happen
Miracle
Right Down to It
Stone Cold Gentleman
Word to the Badd
Reid, Mike
Forever's as Far as I'll Go
Reyes, Franc

Temptation
Rhodes, Taylor
Where Does My Heart Beat Now
Richards, Keith
Highwire
Richman, Jonathan
My Career as a Homewrecker
1963
Ridenhour, Carlton
Bring the Noise
How to Kill a Radio Consultant
Ridgway, Stan
I Wanna Be a Boss
Riley, Teddy
Do Me Right
I Like the Way (The Kissing Game)
Let's Chill
Robbins, Dennis
Two of a Kind, Workin' on a Full
House
Robertson, Robbie
Broken Arrow
Go Back to the Woods
Resurrection
Soapbox Preacher
Robertz, Stuart
How to Kill a Radio Consultant
Robinson, Chris
She Talks to Angels
Robinson, Rich
She Talks to Angels
Robinson, William "Smokey"
The Way You Do the Things You Do
Rockett, Rikki
Something to Believe In
Rodgers, Richard
I'm Talking to My Pal
Rodgers, Ronnie
The Way You Do the Things You Do
Rogers, Evan
Hey Donna
P.A.S.S.I.O.N.
Street of Dreams
Rogers, Norman
Juvenile Delinquintz

# Lyricists & Composers Index

# Lyricists & Composers Index

# Important Performances Index

Songs are listed under the works in which they were introduced or given significant renditions. The index is organized into major sections by performance medium: Album, Movie, Musical, Performer, Revue, Television Show.

## Album

Aces
  Outbound Plane
  Someday Soon

Achtung Baby
  The Fly

After the Rain
  After the Rain

Alias
  Waiting for Love

All American Boy
  War Song

All I Can Be
  Love Me

All Shook Down
  When It Began

Always
  Love Makes Things Happen

Anything Is Possible
  One Hand, One Heart

Apocalypse '91...The Enemy Strikes Back
  How to Kill a Radio Consultant

Assassins
  Everybody's Got the Right (to Their Dreams)
  Gun Song
  I'm Worthy of Your Love

Attack of the Killer B's
  Bring the Noise

B Angie B
  I Don't Wanna Lose Your Love
  So Much Love

Back from Rio
  If We Never Meet Again
  King of the Hill
  Someone to Love

Back to the Grindstone
  Are You Lovin' Me Like I'm Lovin' You

Backdraft
  Set Me in Motion

Backroads
  I Am a Simple Man
  Keep It Between the Lines
  Rockin' Years

Beauty & the Beast
  Be My Guest
  Beauty & the Beast
  Belle

New Jack City
  I Wanna Sex You Up (from *New Jack City*)
  I'm Dreamin' (from *New Jack City*)
New Moon Shine
  Copperline
  Down in the Hole
The New Nashville Cats
  Restless
Nia Peeples
  Street of Dreams
Night Ride Home
  Come in from the Cold
  Ray's Dad's Cadillac
Nights Like This
  Heat of the Moment
No Fences
  The Thunder Rolls
No Rules
  Don't Need Rules
Notorious
  Backlash
Now
  Time after Time
Of the Heart, of the Soul and of the Cross
  Set Adrift on Memory Bliss
On Every Street
  Calling Elvis
1916
  1916
Only Human
  Only Human
Out of Time
  Losing My Religion
  Shiny Happy People
  Texarkana
Partyball
  I Wanna Be a Boss
Pass It on Down
  Down Home
  Forever's as Far as I'll Go
  Here We Are
Past the Point of Rescue
  Small Town Saturday Night
Peaceful Journey
  Now That We Found Love

Places I Have Never Been
  Rite of Spring
  That's Enough for Me
Pornograffiti II
  Hole Hearted
  More Than Words
Positively Phranc
  I'm Not Romantic
  '64 Ford
Power of Love
  Don't Want to be a Fool
  Power of Love/Love Power
Prime of My Life
  Don't Wanna Change the World
Prince of Tides
  Places That Belong to You
Private Line
  Private Line
Put Me in Your Mix
  Put Me in Your Mix
Put Yourself in My Shoes
  Loving Blind
  Where Are You Now
Queen's Logic
  Fooled Around and Fell in Love
Ralph Tresvant
  Do What I Gotta Do
  Sensitivity
  Stone Cold Gentleman
A Real Life Story
  A Family Tie
The Reality of My Surroundings
  So Many Millions
  Sunless Saturday
The Rembrandts
  Just the Way It Is, Baby
The Revival
  Whatever You Want
Rhythm Nation 1814
  Love Will Never Do (Without You)
Ricochet
  Ricochet
Ritual de lo Habitual
  Been Caught Stealing
Ritual of Love
  Romantic

## Movie

125

# Important Performances Index — Performer

# Important Performances Index — Performer

Escape Club
  I'll Be There
Estefan, Gloria
  Coming Out of the Dark
Extreme
  Hole Hearted
  More Than Words
fIREHOSE
  Flyin' the Flannel
Firehouse
  Don't Treat Me Bad
  Love of a Lifetime
Fischer, Lisa
  How Can I Ease the Pain
Fishbone
  So Many Millions
  Sunless Saturday
Flack, Roberta
  Set the Night to Music
Ford, Lita
  Shot of Poison
Fordham, Julia
  (Love Moves in) Mysterious Ways
  Rainbow Heart
Fourplay
  After the Dance
Franks, Michael
  Woman in the Waves
Frey, Glenn
  Part of You, Part of Me
Gabriel, Peter
  Give Peace a Chance
Gang of Four
  FMUSA
  Money Talks
Garber, Victor
  Gun Song
Garfunkel, Art
  Over the Brooklyn Bridge
Garin, Michael
  Never Pay Musicians What They're
    Worth
Genesis
  No Son of Mine
Gerardo
  Rico Suave
  We Want the Funk

Germann, Greg
  I'm Worthy of Your Love
Gibson, Debbie
  One Hand, One Heart
Gillman, Jane
  Song of Baltimore
Gold, Julie
  Fun to Be Perfect
Golden, Annie
  I'm Worthy of Your Love
Grant, Amy
  Baby Baby
  Every Heartbeat
  That's What Love Is For
Griffith, Nanci
  Heaven
  Late Night Grande Hotel
  The Power Lines
Guns N' Roses
  Don't Cry
  Live and Let Die
  November Rain
  You Could Be Mine
Guy
  Do Me Right
  Let's Chill
Hadary, Jonathan
  Gun Song
Hammer
  Addams Groove
  Give Peace a Chance
  2 Legit to Quit
Havens, Richie
  Time after Time
Hawkes, Chesney
  The One and Only (from *Doc
    Hollywood*)
Heavy D and the Boyz
  Now That We Found Love
Hell, Richard, & The Voidoids
  Destiny Street
Henry, Don
  Cadillac Avenue
  Into a Mall
  Mr. God
Hi-Five
  I Can't Wait Another Minute
  I Like the Way (The Kissing Game)

128

## Play

## Revue

## Television Show

# Awards Index

A list of songs nominated for Academy Awards by the Academy of Motion Picture Arts and Sciences and Grammy Awards from the National Academy of Recording Arts and Sciences. Asterisks indicate the winners.

## 1991

Academy Award
  Be My Guest
  Beauty & the Beast*
  Belle
  (Everything I Do) I Do It for You
    (from *Robin Hood*)
Grammy Award
  Baby Baby
  Been Caught Stealing
  Can You Stop the Rain?
  Can't Stop This Thing We Started
  Don't Rock the Jukebox
  Down at the Twist and Shout
  Eagle When She Flies
  Enter Sandman
  Gotta Have You
  Here's a Quarter (Call Someone Who
    Cares)
  How Can I Ease the Pain

(Everything I Do) I Do It for You
  (from *Robin Hood*)
(Everything I Do) I Do It for You
  (from *Robin Hood*)*
I Wanna Sex You Up (from *New
  Jack City*)
I'll Take You There
Jungle Fever
Learning to Fly
Losing My Religion
Love Can Build a Bridge*
Power of Love/Love Power*
Silent Lucidity
Something to Talk About
Somewhere in My Memory (from
  *Home Alone*)
The Soul Cages*
Unforgettable*
Walking in Memphis
You Can't Resist It

# List of Publishers

A directory of publishers of the songs included in *Popular Music,* 1991. Publishers that are members of the American Society of Composers, Authors, and Publishers or whose catalogs are available under ASCAP license are indicated by the designation (ASCAP). Publishers that have granted performing rights to Broadcast Music, Inc., are designated by the notation (BMI). Publishers whose catalogs are represented by SESAC, Inc., are indicated by the designation (SESAC).

The addresses were gleaned from a variety of sources, including ASCAP, BMI, SESAC, *Billboard* magazine, and the National Music Publishers' Association. As in any volatile industry, many of the addresses may become outdated quickly. In the interim between the book's completion and its subsequent publication, some publishers may have been consolidated into others or changed hands. This is a fact of life long endured by the music business and its constituents. The data collected here, and throughout the book, are as accurate as such circumstances allow.

## A

ABCDE (ASCAP)
see MCA, Inc.

Ackee Music Inc. (ASCAP)
see Island Music

Across 110th Street (ASCAP)
c/o SBK Songs
1290 Avenue of the Americas
New York, New York 10019

Acuff-Rose Publications Inc. (BMI)
2510 Franklin Road
Nashville, Tennessee 37204

Aerostation Corp. (ASCAP)
16214 Morrison Street
Encino, California 91436

Affirmative (BMI)
see WB Music Corp.

Age to Age (ASCAP)
see MCA, Inc.

AGF Music Ltd. (ASCAP)
1500 Broadway, Suite 2805
New York, New York 10036

Air Bear (BMI)
c/o Warner-Tamerlane
9000 Sunset Blvd.
Los Angeles, California 90069

Alabama Band Music Co. (ASCAP)
803 18th Avenue S.
Nashville, Tennessee 37203

# List of Publishers

Alamo Music, Inc. (ASCAP)
1619 Broadway, 11th Fl.
New York, New York 10019

All Nations Music (ASCAP)
8857 W. Blvd., Suite 200
Beverly Hills; California 90211

Almo Music Corp. (ASCAP)
1416 N. La Brea Avenue
Hollywood, California 90028

American Made Music (BMI)
c/o Little Big Town Music
803 18th Avenue, S.
Nashville, Tennessee 37203

Andi Beat Goes On (BMI)
see EMI Music Publishing, Ltd.

Anna Gate (BMI)
Address Unavailable

April First (ASCAP)
c/o Camilla McGuinn
P.O. Box 5437
Indian Rocks Beach, Florida 34635

Arc Music Corp. (BMI)
c/o The Goodman Group
110 E. 59th Street
New York, New York 10022

Arista Music, Inc.
8370 Wilshire Blvd.
Beverly Hills, California 90211

Aron Gate (BMI)
see MCA, Inc.

ATV Music Corp. (BMI)
c/o ATV Group
6255 Sunset Blvd.
Hollywood, California 90028

Automatic Street
Address Unavailable

Ayesha (ASCAP)
see Warner-Chappell Music

Azmah Eel (ASCAP)
see Me Good

# B

B. Funk (ASCAP)
see Warner-Chappell Music

Back to Mono Music Inc. (BMI)
c/o Phil Spector
P.O. Box 69529
Los Angeles, California 90069

Badams (ASCAP)
see Almo Music Corp.

Bait and Beer (ASCAP)
c/o Terrell Tye
P.O. Box 120657
Nashville, Tennessee 37212

Denise Barry Music (ASCAP)
c/o Peter T. Paterno, Esq.
Manatt, Phelps, Rothenberg & Tunney
11355 W. Olympic Blvd.
Los Angeles, California 90064

Basement Boys (BMI)
see Polygram Music Publishing Inc.

Basically Gasp Music (ASCAP)
115 Ivy Drive, No. 10
Charlottesville, Virginia 22901

Bass Hit (ASCAP)
723 7th Avenue
12th Floor
New York, New York 10016

Bayjun Beat (BMI)
see MCA Music

Beau Di O Do Music (BMI)
c/o Warner-Tamerlane Pub. Co.
9000 Sunset Blvd., Penthouse
Los Angeles, California 90069

Been Jammin' Music (BMI)
c/o J. Greco
63 St. Marks Place, No. 4B
New York City, New York 10003

Beeswing Music (BMI)
c/o Gary Stamler
2029 Century Park, E., Suite 1500
Los Angeles, California 90067

Behind Bars (ASCAP)
Thiele
149 1/2 South Palm Drive
Beverly Hills, California 90212

Belwin-Mills Publishing Corp. (ASCAP)
1776 Broadway, 11th Fl.
New York, New York 10019

Benefit (BMI)

Benny's Music (BMI)
see EMI-Blackwood Music Inc.

Berrios (ASCAP)
see Cutting Music

Betdolph Music (ASCAP)
see Notable Music Co., Inc.

Bethlehem (BMI)
see EMI-Blackwood Music Inc.

Bibo Music Publishers (ASCAP)
see Welk Music Group

Big Sky Music (ASCAP)
P.O. Box 860, Cooper Sta.
New York, New York 10276

Big Three Music Corp.
729 Seventh Avenue
New York, New York 10019

Big Toots Tunes
Address Unavailable

Black Sheep Music Inc. (BMI)
see Screen Gems-EMI Music Inc.

Black Stallion County Publishing (BMI)
P.O. Box 368
Tujunga, California 91043-036

Bleu Disque Music (ASCAP)
c/o Warner Brothers Music
9000 Sunset Blvd., Penthouse
Los Angeles, California 90069

Blue Turtle (ASCAP)
see Magnetic

Blues Traveler
see Irving Music Inc.

BMG Music (ASCAP)
1133 Sixth Avenue
New York, New York 10036

BMG Songs Inc. (ASCAP)
1133 Avenue of the Americas
New York, New York 10036

Bob-a-Lew Songs (ASCAP)
P.O. Box 8031
Universal City, California 91608

Body Electric Music (BMI)
see WB Music Corp.

Bon Jovi Publishing (ASCAP)
see PRI Music

Bona Relations Music (BMI)
see WB Music Corp.

Emily Boothe (BMI)
2910 Poston Ave.
Nashville, Tennessee 37203

Bouillabaisse Music (BMI)
see MCA, Inc.

Bourne Co. (ASCAP)
437 Fifth Avenue
New York, New York 10016

Braintree Music (BMI)
c/o Segel & Goldman Inc.
9348 Santa Monica Blvd., No. 304
Beverly Hills, California 90210

Brass & Chance (ASCAP)
see MCA, Inc.

Bridgeport Music Inc. (BMI)
c/o Norman R. Kurtz
712 Fifth Avenue
New York, New York 10019

Brio Blues (ASCAP)
see Almo Music Corp.

Broadhead (BMI)
see WB Music Corp.

Brogue Music (BMI)
see WB Music Corp.

Brown/Feldman (ASCAP)
P.O. Box 4044
St. Paul, Minnesota 55104

Bruised Oranges (ASCAP)
c/o Sy Miller
565 Fifth Avenue, Suite 1001
New York, New York 10017

Bubbly Orange Stuff (BMI)
see WB Music Corp.

Budsky (BMI)
see Zuri

Buffalo (ASCAP)
see EMI-April Music Inc.

Bug Music (BMI)
Bug Music Group
6777 Hollywood Blvd., 9th Fl.
Hollywood, California 90028

Burbank Plaza (ASCAP)
c/o Filmtrax Copyright Holdings
3808 Riverside Dr.
Burbank, California 91505

Bush Burnin' Music (ASCAP)
1020 Grand Concourse, Suite 17W
Bronx, New York 10451

Bust It Publishing (BMI)
c/o Manatt Phelps and Phillips
11355 W. Olympic Blvd.
Los Angeles, California 90064

## C

John Cafferty Music (BMI)
c/o Arnold Freedman
1200 Providence Hwy.
Sharon, Massachusetts 02067

Cal Cody
see Wee B Music

Caledonia Productions (ASCAP)
see WB Music Corp.

Calogie Music (ASCAP)
see Warner-Chappell Music

Captain Z (ASCAP)
see Almo Music Corp.

Careers-BMG
see BMG Music

Careers Music Inc. (ASCAP)
see Arista Music, Inc.

M. Carey Songs
see Sony Songs

Carlooney Tunes (ASCAP)
see Chrysalis Music Corp.

Carnelia Music (ASCAP)
see A. Schroeder International Ltd.

CBS/Epic/Solar
see Kear Music

Cedarwood Publishing Co., Inc. (BMI)
39 Music Square, E.
Nashville, Tennessee 37203

Chappell & Co., Inc. (ASCAP)
810 Seventh Avenue
New York, New York 10019

Chariscourt Ltd. (ASCAP)
see Almo Music Corp.

Charm Trap Music (BMI)
see EMI-Blackwood Music Inc.

Cherry Lane Music Co., Inc. (ASCAP)
110 Midland Avenue
Port Chester, New York 10573

Chi-Boy (ASCAP)
c/o Schwartz & Farquharson
9107 Wilshire Blvd., Suite 300
Beverly Hills, California 90216

Christ & Co. (BMI)
see Bug Music

Chrysalis Music Corp. (ASCAP)
Chrysalis Music Group
645 Madison Avenue
New York, New York 10022

Cole-Clivilles (ASCAP)
see Virgin Music, Inc.

Colgems-EMI Music Inc. (ASCAP)
see Screen Gems-EMI Music Inc.

Tom Collins Music Corp. (BMI)
P.O. Box 121407
Nashville, Tennessee 37212

Controversy Music (ASCAP)
c/o Manatt, Phelps, Rothenberg
Att: Lee Phillips
11355 W. Olympic Blvd.
Los Angeles, California 90064

Convee
see Lynn Jacobs Publishing

142

Copyright Control (ASCAP)
see Bug Music

Copyright Management Inc. (BMI)
1102 17th Ave So.
Nashville, Tennessee 37082

Core Music Publishing (BMI)
c/o Oak Manor
Box 1000
Oak Ridges, Ontario
Canada

Corina Starr Music (ASCAP)

Cornelios Carlos (ASCAP)
see MCA, Inc.

Cosby & Ellis (ASCAP)
see Sony Tunes

Could Be Music (BMI)
see MCA Music

Country Road Music Inc. (BMI)
c/o Gelfand, Rennert & Feldman
Att: Babbie Green
1880 Century Park, E., No. 900
Los Angeles, California 90067

Crabshaw Music (ASCAP)
3875 19th Street
San Francisco, California 94114

Crazy Crow Music (BMI)
see Siquomb Publishing Corp.

Creeping Death Music (ASCAP)
see Cherry Lane Music Co., Inc.

CRGI (BMI)
c/o CBS (Sony Records)
666 5th Ave.
New York City, New York 10103

Criterion Music Corp. (ASCAP)
6124 Selma Avenue
Hollywood, California 90028

Cross Keys Publishing Co., Inc. (ASCAP)
see Tree Publishing Co., Inc.

Cutting Music (ASCAP)
111 Dyckman Street
New York, New York 10040

Cyanide (BMI)
see Willesden Music, Inc.

# D

D 'N' A (BMI)
see BMG Music

Da Braddah's (BMI)
see EMI-Blackwood Music Inc.

Da Posse's (BMI)
see WB Music Corp.

Daksel Music Corp. (BMI)
c/o Leber and Krebs Inc.
65 W. 55th Street
New York, New York 10019

Dancing Teen (BMI)
see Duke T

Deborah Anne's Music (ASCAP)
1684 Sterling Avenue
Merrick, New York 11566

Deco Music (BMI)
see MCA, Inc.

Def American Songs (BMI)
298 Elizabeth Street
New York, New York 10012

Def Jam (ASCAP)
5 University Place
New York, New York 10003

Def USA (BMI)
see Def American Songs

Dejamus California (ASCAP)
see Dick James Music Inc.

Del Sounds Music (BMI)
c/o Happy Valley Music
1 Camp Street
Cambridge, Massachusetts 02140

Desmobile Music Co. (ASCAP)
Att: Desmond Child
12 W. 72nd Street
New York, New York 10023

Deswing Mob (ASCAP)
see EMI-April Music Inc.

Donna Dijon Music (BMI)
see Zevon Music Inc.

Dinger & Ollie (BMI)
see Duke T

Walt Disney Music Co. (ASCAP)
350 S. Buena Vista Street
Burbank, California 91521

Diva One (ASCAP)
Gelfand, Rennert & Feldman
c/o Michael Bivens
1880 Century Park East, Ste. 900
Los Angeles, California 90067

Diva 1 Music (ASCAP)
see Spectrum VII

Dixie Stars (ASCAP)
see MCA, Inc.

Donnie D. (ASCAP)
see Warner-Chappell Music

Donril Music (ASCAP)
see Zomba House

Dick Dragon Music (BMI)
see Virgin Music, Inc.

Drumlin Ltd. (England)
Address Unavailable

Druse Music Inc. (ASCAP)
c/o Meibach & Epstein
680 Fifth Avenue, Suite 500
New York, New York 10019

Dub Notes (ASCAP)
c/o Levine & Thall, PC
485 Madison Avenue
New York, New York 10022

Duchess Music Corp. (BMI)
see MCA Music

Duke T (BMI)
11355 W. Olympic Blvd.
Los Angeles, California 90064

Dwaine Duane (BMI)
Address Unavailable

Dyad Music, Ltd. (BMI)
c/o Mason & Co.
75 Rockefeller Plaza
New York, New York 10019

Dynatone (BMI)
see Unichappell Music Inc.

# E

E/A (BMI)
c/o Warner-Tamerlane
9000 Sunset Blvd.
Los Angeles, California 90069

E-Z Duz It (ASCAP)
see Zomba House

Barry Eastmond Music (ASCAP)
400 E. 17th Street
New York, New York 11226

Eden Bridge Music (ASCAP)
Address Unavailable

Edge o' the Woods (ASCAP)
1214 16th Ave. South
Nashville, Tennessee 37212

Edisto Sound International (BMI)
see CRGI

Editions EG (ASCAP)
9157 Sunset Blvd. Suite 215
Los Angeles, California 90069

Edward Grant (ASCAP)
2910 Poston Ave.
Nashville, Tennessee 37203

E.G. Music, Inc. (BMI)
161 W. 54th Street
New York, New York 10019

Electric Mule (BMI)
see Tree Publishing Co., Inc.

E.M. Marl
see Marley Marl

Emanuel Music (ASCAP)
c/o Breslauer, Jacobson & Rutman
10880 Wilshire Blvd., Suite 2110
Los Angeles, California 90024

Embryotic (BMI)
see WB Music Corp.

EMI April Canada

EMI-April Music Inc. (ASCAP)
49 E. 52nd Street
New York, New York 10022

EMI-Blackwood Music Inc. (BMI)
   1350 Avenue of the Americas
   23rd Fl.
   New York, New York 10019

EMI Unart Catalogue
   Address Unavailable

End of Music (BMI)
   see Virgin Music, Inc.

Enough to Contend With (BMI)
   see Def American Songs

Ensign Music Corp. (BMI)
   c/o Sidney Herman
   1 Gulf & Western Plaza
   New York, New York 10023

Epic/Solar (BMI)
   see Kear Music

Esta Chica (BMI)

Even Stevens (BMI)
   Address Unavailable


# F

Fall Line Orange Music (ASCAP)
   1880 Century Park E., No. 900
   Los Angeles, California 90067

Famous Monsters Music (BMI)
   140 E. Seventh Street
   New York, New York 10009

Famous Music Corp. (ASCAP)
   Gulf & Western Industries, Inc.
   1 Gulf & Western Plaza
   New York, New York 10023

Mike Ferguson Music Co. (BMI)
   3378 Clayton Blvd.
   Shaker Heights, Ohio 44120

Fiction Music Inc. (BMI)
   P.O. Box 135
   Bearsville, New York 12409

Fiddleback Music Publishing Co., Inc. (BMI)
   1270 Avenue of the Americas
   New York, New York 10020

Fifth Floor Music Inc. (ASCAP)
   Att: Martin Cohen
   6430 Sunset Blvd., Suite 1500
   Los Angeles, California 90028

Fifth to March (BMI)
   see WB Music Corp.

Flip-a-Jig (ASCAP)
   Address Unavailable

Flyte Tyme Tunes (ASCAP)
   c/o Avant Garde Music Publishing
   9229 Sunset Blvd., Suite 311
   Los Angeles, California 90069

Folkswim
   Address Unavailable

Foon Tunes (BMI)
   see WB Music Corp.

Foreign Imported (BMI)
   8921 S.W. Tenth Terrace
   Miami, Florida 33174

Forerunner (ASCAP)
   P.O. Box 120657
   Nashville, Tennessee 37212

Forrest Hills Music Inc. (BMI)
   1609 Hawkins Street
   Nashville, Tennessee 37203

Fort Knox Music Co. (BMI)
   see Hudson Bay Music Co.

4MW (ASCAP)
   see Zomba House

Fox Film Music Corp. (BMI)
   c/o Twentieth Century Fox Film Corp
   P.O. Box 900
   Beverly Hills, California 90213

Full Keel (ASCAP)
   4450 Lakeside Dr., Ste. 200
   Burbank, California 91505

Funky Metal (ASCAP)
   see Almo Music Corp.

Funzalo Music (BMI)
   225 W. 57th Street
   New York, New York 10019

# List of Publishers

## G

Gale Warnings (BMI)
see Hiss N' Tell

Galeneye (BMI)
see Acuff-Rose Publications Inc.

Gangsta Boogie (ASCAP)
see Chappell & Co., Inc.

Geffen Again Music (BMI)
see Geffen Music

Geffen Music (ASCAP)
see MCA, Inc.

Gerard Video (BMI)
see WB Music Corp.

Getarealjob Music (ASCAP)
c/o Studio One Artists
P.O. Box 5824
Bethesda, Maryland 20814

GG Loves Music (BMI)
see WB Music Corp.

Beverly Glen Publishing (ASCAP)
c/o Loeb and Loeb
Att: D. Thompson
10100 Santa Monica Blvd.
Suite 2200
Los Angeles, California 90067

Goldline Music Inc. (ASCAP)
see Silverline Music, Inc.

Julie Gold's Music (BMI)
see Irving Music Inc.

Michael H. Goldsen, Inc. (ASCAP)
6124 Selma Avenue
Hollywood, California 90028

Gone Gator Music (ASCAP)
c/o Bernard Gudvi & Co., Inc.
6420 Wilshire Blvd., Suite 425
Los Angeles, California 90048

Googiplex (BMI)
see WB Music Corp.

Gorno Music (ASCAP)
c/o Alan N. Skiena, Esq.
1775 Broadway
New York, New York 10007

Grand Illusion Music (ASCAP)
see Almo Music Corp.

Grandma Annie Music (BMI)
c/o Sy Miller, Esq.
18 E. 48th Street, Suite 1202
New York, New York 10017

Grandma's Hands (BMI)
see WB Music Corp.

Gratitude Sky Music, Inc. (ASCAP)
c/o Gelfand
2062 Union Street
San Francisco, California 94123

Green Linnet Records (BMI)
43 Beaver Brook Rd.
Danbury, Connecticut 06810

Al Green Music Inc. (BMI)
3208 Winchester Road
Memphis, Tennessee 38118

Green Skirt Music (BMI)
see Kear Music

Grey Dog Music (ASCAP)
c/o Pryor, Cashman & Sherman
410 Park Avenue
New York, New York 10022

Guns N' Roses Music (ASCAP)
see Cherry Lane Music Co., Inc.

Gunster (ASCAP)
see EMI-April Music Inc.

## H

H-Naja (BMI)
H Management
317 N. Broad St.
Philadelphia, Pennsylvania 19107

Rick Hall Music (ASCAP)
P.O. Box 2527
603 E. Avalon Avenue
Muscle Shoals, Alabama 35662

Hampstead Heath Music Publishers Ltd.
(ASCAP)
7505 Jerez Court, Suite E
Rancho La Costa
Carlsbad, California 92008

Haverstraw (ASCAP)

Hayes Street (ASCAP)
see Almo Music Corp.

Heartland Express (ASCAP)
see EMI-April Music Inc.

Hi-Frost

Hidden Pun (BMI)
1841 Broadway
New York, New York 10023

Hilmer Music Publishing Co. (ASCAP)
see Almo Music Corp.

Himmasongs (ASCAP)
Address Unavailable

Hip Hop (BMI)
870 Seventh Ave., 30th Fl.
New York, New York 10019

Hip-Trip Music Co. (BMI)
c/o Glen E. Davis
1635 N. Cahuenga Blvd., 6th Fl.
Hollywood, California 90028

Hiss N' Tell (ASCAP)
84 47th St.
Astoria, New York 11103

Hit List (ASCAP)
The Music Group
40 W. 57th St. Ste. 1515
New York, New York 10019

HLN (ASCAP)
see Hulex Music

Howie Tee (BMI)
see Irving Music Inc.

Howlin' Hits Music (ASCAP)
P.O. Box 19647
Houston, Texas 77224

Hudson Bay Music Co. (BMI)
1619 Broadway, Suite 906
New York, New York 10019

Hulex Music (BMI)
P.O. Box 819
Mill Valley, California 94942

Hummasongs (ASCAP)
see Warner-Chappell Music

# I

ICBD (BMI)
see MCA, Inc.

Ice Baby

Ice Nine Publishing Co., Inc. (ASCAP)
P.O. Box 1073
San Rafael, California 94915

Ides of March Music Division (ASCAP)
Wayfield Inc.
1136 Gateway Lane
Nashville, Tennessee 37220

Ignorant (ASCAP)
see Warner-Chappell Music

I'll Hit You Back (BMI)
see WB Music Corp.

Illegal Songs, Inc. (BMI)
c/o Beverly Martin
633 N. La Brea Avenue
Hollywood, California 90036

Intersong, USA Inc.
c/o Chappell & Co., Inc.
810 Seventh Avenue
New York, New York 10019

I.R.S. (BMI)
Address Unavailable

Irving Music Inc. (BMI)
1358 N. La Brea
Hollywood, California 90028

Chris Isaak Music Publishing (ASCAP)
P.O. Box 547
Larkspur, California 94939

Island Music (BMI)
c/o Mr. Lionel Conway
6525 Sunset Blvd.
Hollywood, California 90028

# J

Lynn Jacobs Publishing (BMI)
24747 W. Calle Altamina
Calabasas, California 91302

# List of Publishers

Dick James Music Inc. (BMI)
24 Music Square, E.
Nashville, Tennessee 37203

Jamm (ASCAP)
Address Unavailable

Jessie Joe (BMI)

Jetydosa (BMI)
see Island Music

Jobete Music Co., Inc. (ASCAP)
Att: Erlinda N. Barrios
6255 Sunset Blvd., Suite 1600
Hollywood, California 90028

Joelsongs (BMI)
see EMI-April Music Inc.

JRM (ASCAP)
see EMI-April Music Inc.

Juicy
Address Unavailable

Juters Publishing Co. (BMI)
c/o Funzalo Music
Att: Mike's Management
445 Park Avenue, 7th Fl.
New York, New York 10022

# K

K-Shreve (ASCAP)
see EMI-April Music Inc.

Kallman Music, Inc. (ASCAP)
Div. of Hands on Productions
19 W. 21st St.
New York, New York 10010

Hilary Kanter (BMI)
Address Unavailable

Kear Music (BMI)
Division of La Face, Inc.
c/o Carter Turner & Co.
9229 Sunset Blvd.
Los Angeles, California 90069

Pam Jo Keen (BMI)
see EMI-Blackwood Music Inc.

Keep Your Music (ASCAP)
Bilal, Brown & Williams
c/o Vernon Brown
555 White Plains Road
Tarrytown, New York 10591

Kinetic Diamond (ASCAP)
513 Hill Road
Nashville, Tennessee 37220

King Reyes (ASCAP)
see Cutting Music

Kings Kid (BMI)
see WB Music Corp.

Stephen A. Kipner (ASCAP)
see Warner-Chappell Music

Kokomo Music (ASCAP)
Att: Bonnie Raitt
P.O. Box 626
Los Angeles, California 90078

# L

La Sab (BMI)
see H-Naja

Lagunatic Music (ASCAP)
see Virgin Music, Inc.

Lamartine (ASCAP)
see Lost Lake Arts Music

Lambardoni Edizioni (ASCAP)
see Intersong, USA Inc.

Sidney Lawrence Company
Address Unavailable

Jerry Leiber Music (ASCAP)
1619 Broadway, 11th Fl.
New York, New York 10019

Leibraphone (ASCAP)
see Polygram Music Publishing Inc.

Lenono Music (BMI)
The Studio
1 W. 72nd Street
New York, New York 10023

Leo Sun (ASCAP)
see EMI-April Music Inc.

Leprechaun Music (ASCAP)
Address Unavailable

Levine & Brown Music Inc. (BMI)
c/o Arrow, Edelstein & Gross
Att: John Gross, Esq.
919 Third Avenue
New York, New York 10022

Lew-Bob Songs (BMI)
P.O. Box 8031
Universal City, California 91608

Lexor (ASCAP)
see Warner-Chappell Music

Linda's Boys Music (BMI)
see WB Music Corp.

Lion Hearted Music
see EMI-April Music Inc.

Lisabella Music (ASCAP)
see Cherry Lane Music Co., Inc.

Little Big Town Music (BMI)
see Jessie Joe

Little Jake (ASCAP)
Address Unavailable

Little Nemo (ASCAP)
c/o Almo
1416 N. Labrea Avenue
Los Angeles, California 90028

L.L. Cool J Music (ASCAP)
see Def Jam

London (BMI)
Address Unavailable

Long Run Music Co., Inc. (BMI)
see WB Music Corp.

Longitude Music (BMI)
c/o Windswept Pacific Entertainment
Co.
4450 Lakeside Drive, Suite 200
Burbank, California 91505

Lost Lake Arts Music (ASCAP)
Div. of Windham Hill Productions
831 High Street
Palo Alto, California 94301

Louis St. (BMI)
4945 Whitsett, No. 4
North Hollywood, California 91607

Love Pump
Address Unavailable

Love Tone (ASCAP)
1925 Century Park East, Ste. 1260
Los Angeles, California 90067

Lyle Lovett (ASCAP)
c/o Michael H. Goldsen Inc.
6124 Selma Avenue
Hollywood, California 90028

Luck Skillet Music (ASCAP)
see Almo Music Corp.

Lucrative (BMI)
P.O. Box 90363
Nashville, Tennessee 37209

# M

Maanami (ASCAP)
see EMI-April Music Inc.

Macadamian (ASCAP)
see Geffen Music

Maclen Music Inc. (BMI)
see ATV Music Corp.

Macy Place Music (ASCAP)
see WB Music Corp.

Maestro B. (ASCAP)
see Warner-Chappell Music

Magnified (ASCAP)
see Warner-Chappell Music

Main Lot (BMI)
1416 N. La Brea Ave.
Hollywood, California 90028

Major Bob Music (ASCAP)
1109 17th Avenue South
Nashville, Tennessee 37212

Mambadaddi (BMI)
5606 Bennett Avenue
Austin, Texas 78751

# List of Publishers

Man-Ken Music Ltd. (BMI)
    34 Pheasant Run
    Old Westbury, New York 11568

M&T Spencer (ASCAP)
    1925 Century Park East, Ste. 1260
    Los Angeles, California 90067

March 9 Music (ASCAP)
    c/o Garey, Mason, Sloane
    1299 Ocean Avenue, Penthouse
    Santa Monica, California 90401

Mariah Songs (BMI)
    see Sony Songs

Marion Place
    see BMG Music

Marjer Publishing
    see Stage-Screen Music, Inc.

Market Music (ASCAP)
    see EMI-April Music Inc.

Marky Mark (BMI)
    see WB Music Corp.

Marley Marl (ASCAP)
    Marl International
    48 Lawrence Place
    Chestnut Ridge, New York 10977

Bob Marley Music, Ltd. (ASCAP)
    c/o David J. Steinberg, Esq.
    Rita Marley Music Division
    North American Bldg., 20th Fl.
    121 S. Broad Street
    Philadelphia, Pennsylvania 19107

Marrs Songs Ltd.
    Address Unavailable

Matt-Black (ASCAP)
    see EMI-April Music Inc.

Mattie Ruth (ASCAP)
    1010 16th Ave. South
    Nashville, Tennessee 37212

Maypop Music (BMI)
    Att: Maggie Cavender
    803 18th Avenue, S.
    Nashville, Tennessee 37203

MCA, Inc. (ASCAP)
    c/o Mr. John McKellen
    445 Park Avenue
    New York, New York 10022

MCA Music (ASCAP)
    Division of MCA Inc.
    445 Park Avenue
    New York, New York 10022

McDonald Music Co. (BMI)
    P.O. Box 3316
    San Francisco, California 94116

McGuinn Music (BMI)
    c/o Roger McGuinn
    P.O. Box 5437
    Indian Rocks Beach, Florida 33535

McNally (ASCAP)
    Address Unavailable

Me Good (ASCAP)
    15 Remsen Ave.
    Roslyn, New York 11576

Meat Puppets (BMI)
    Box 110
    Tempe, Arizona 85281

Medicine Hat Music (ASCAP)
    c/o Gelfand, Rennert & Feldman
    Att: Babbie Green
    1880 Century Park, E., No. 900
    Los Angeles, California 90067

Melonie (ASCAP)
    see MCA, Inc.

MHC Music (ASCAP)
    c/o Bug Music
    6777 Hollywood Blvd., 9th Fl.
    Hollywood, California 90028

Midnight Ocean Bonfire (BMI)
    see Irving Music Inc.

Mijac Music (BMI)
    c/o Warner Tamerlane
    Publishing Corp.
    900 Sunset Blvd., Penthouse
    Los Angeles, California 90069

Mike Ten (BMI)
    see Diva One

Millhouse (BMI)
see Welk Music Group

Milsap (BMI)
12 Music Circle, S.
Nashville, Tennessee 37203

Miss Bessie (ASCAP)
see Warner-Chappell Music

Mississippi Mud (BMI)
see WB Music Corp.

Mr. Bolton's Music (BMI)
c/o David Feinstein
120 E. 34th Street, Suite 7F
New York, New York 10011

Mo' Ritmo (ASCAP)
see EMI-April Music Inc.

Mole Hole Music (BMI)
c/o Bug Music Group
6777 Hollywood Blvd., 9th Fl.
Hollywood, California 90028

Moline Valley (ASCAP)
2132 No. Tremont
Chicago, Illinois 60614

Mondo Spartacus Music (BMI)
see Criterion Music Corp.

C. Montrose S.
see Sony Songs

Moo Maison (ASCAP)
see MCA, Inc.

Mopage (BMI)
Address Unavailable

Moriel (BMI)
see Beverly Glen Publishing

Edwin H. Morris

Steveland Morris Music (ASCAP)
4616 Magnolia Boulevard
Burbank, California 91505

Van Morrison (ASCAP)
see Warner-Chappell Music

MPL Communications Inc. (ASCAP)
c/o Lee Eastman
39 W. 54th Street
New York, New York 10019

Muhlenberg: World Wide Music, Inc. (BMI)
see World Wide Music Co., Ltd.

Nick Mundy (BMI)
see WB Music Corp.

Murrah (BMI)
1025 16th Ave. South, Ste. 102
P.O. Box 121623
Nashville, Tennessee 37212

Museum Steps Music (ASCAP)
Gelfand, Rennert & Feldman
6 E. 43rd St.
New York, New York 10017

Music Corp. of America (BMI)
see MCA, Inc.

Mustaine Music (BMI)
see Screen Gems-EMI Music Inc.

Mya-T (BMI)
see Saja Music Co.

# N

NAH Music (ASCAP)
c/o Levine & Epstein
485 Madison Avenue
New York, New York 10022

National League Music (BMI)
6255 Sunset Blvd., Suite 1126
Los Angeles, California 90028

Naughty (ASCAP)
see Jobete Music Co., Inc.

New Hidden Valley Music Co. (ASCAP)
c/o Ernst & Whinney
1875 Century Park, E., No. 2200
Los Angeles, California 90067

New Jersey Underground
see Bon Jovi Publishing

Randy Newman Music (ASCAP)
c/o Gelfand, Rennert & Feldman
1880 Century Park, E., Suite 900
Los Angeles, California 90067

Newton House Music (ASCAP)
c/o E.G. Music
9157 Sunset Blvd.
Los Angeles, California 90069

Next Plateau Entertainment (ASCAP)
730 Fifth Avenue, 9th Floor
New York, New York 10019

NFP (ASCAP)
see Zomba House

Night Garden Music (BMI)
c/o Unichappell Music, Inc.
810 Seventh Avenue, 32nd Fl.
New York, New York 10019

No Chapeau (ASCAP)
see Warner-Chappell Music

No Rules (BMI)
11355 W. Olympic Blvd.
Los Angeles, California 90064

Nonpariel Music (ASCAP)
see Walden Music, Inc.

Northern Music Co.
Address Unavailable

Notable Music Co., Inc. (ASCAP)
Cy Coleman Enterprises
200 W. 54th Street
New York, New York 10019

Number 9 Music (ASCAP)
459 El Camino Drive
Beverly Hills, California 90212

# O

Oakfield Avenue Music Ltd. (BMI)
c/o David Gotterer
Mason & Co.
75 Rockefeller Plaza, Suite 1800
New York, New York 10019

Obie Diner (BMI)
see EMI-April Music Inc.

One Note Publishing (BMI)
see Sawgrass Music

One-Two (BMI)
c/o Tuhin Roy
8265 Sunset Blvd.
Los Angeles, California 90046

Oobe (BMI)
see No Rules

Orion Music Publising (ASCAP)
see Next Plateau Entertainment

O'Ryan Music, Inc (ASCAP)
2910 Poston Ave
Nashville, Tennessee 37203

Otherwise Publishing (ASCAP)
c/o Mark Tanner
1009 Ninth Street, Suite 3
Santa Monica, California 90403

# P

Partner (BMI)
see Polygram Music Publishing Inc.

Paul & Jonathan Songs (BMI)
1330 Dog Creek
Kingston Springs, Tennessee 37082

Paul Craft (BMI)
see Copyright Management Inc.

Peasantmart (ASCAP)
D. Erickson
Rt. 4, Box 428A
Park Rapids, Minnesota 56470

Peer-Southern Organization
1740 Broadway
New York, New York 10019

Peer Talbot (BMI)
see Peer-Southern Organization

Personal Music (ASCAP)
see BMG Music

Pertaining To Music (BMI)
P.O. Box 158
Arvonia, Virginia 23004

Pettibone (ASCAP)
see Kear Music

Phantom (ASCAP)
see Warner-Chappell Music

Phonogram
see Polygram Songs

Pine Barrens Music (BMI)
c/o Fred Small
80 Aberdeen Avenue
Cambridge, Massachusetts 02138

Pitchford (BMI)
1880 Century Park
Los Angeles, California 90067

Pokazuka (ASCAP)
see Alamo Music, Inc.

Polygram International (ASCAP)
see Polygram Music Publishing Inc.

Polygram Music Publishing Inc. (ASCAP)
Att: Brian Kelleher
c/o Polygram Records Inc.
810 Seventh Avenue
New York, New York 10019

PolyGram Records Inc. (ASCAP)
810 Seventh Avenue
New York, New York 10019

Polygram Songs (BMI)
810 Seventh Avenue
New York, New York 10019

Ponder Heart Music (BMI)
see Irving Music Inc.

Pookie's Music (BMI)
see EMI-Blackwood Music Inc.

Posey Publishing (BMI)
412 Oakleigh Hill
Nashville, Tennessee 37215

Post Oak (BMI)
see Tree Publishing Co., Inc.

PRI Music (ASCAP)
810 7th Ave.
New York City, New York 10019

Promopub BV
Address Unavailable

Promostraat

Pronto Music, Inc. (BMI)
see WB Music Corp.

Pterodactyl (BMI)
see Green Linnet Records

Public Domain

Pundit
see Springtime Music Inc.

# Q

QPM (ASCAP)
see EMI-April Music Inc.

Quaker Oats, Inc.
Address Unavailable

Queen Latifah (ASCAP)
Address Unavailable

Quinvy Music Publishing Co. (BMI)
see WB Music Corp.

# R

Rada Dara Music (BMI)
c/o Donald Rubin
29775 Pacific Coast Hwy.
Zuma Beach, California 90265

Ramal Music Co. (BMI)
5999 Bear Creek Rd. No. 304
Bedford Heights, Ohio 44146

Ranch Rock (ASCAP)
see Warner-Chappell Music

Ranger Bob Music (ASCAP)
1299 Ocean Avenue, Suite 800
Santa Monica, California 90401

Re-Deer (ASCAP)
2428 Kent Village Place
Landover, Maryland 20785

Really Useful Group (ASCAP)
see Screen Gems-EMI Music Inc.

Realsongs (ASCAP)
Address Unavailable

Reata Publishing Inc. (ASCAP)
9000 Sunset Blvd.
Los Angeles, California 90069

Rebel Larynx (BMI)
Gary Stamler Mgmt.
2029 Century Pk. E., Ste. 1500
Los Angeles, California 90067

Red Linnet (BMI)
see Green Linnet Records

Red Rubber (ASCAP)

Reformation Publishing USA
c/o Robbins Spielman Slayton & Co.
1700 Broadway
New York, New York 10019

Reilla Music Corp. (BMI)
c/o Joseph E. Zynczak
65 W. 55th Street, No. 4G
New York, New York 10019

Reunion (ASCAP)
see EMI-April Music Inc.

Revelation Music Publishing Corp. (ASCAP)
Tommy Valando Publishing Group Inc.
1270 Avenue of the Americas
Suite 2110
New York, New York 10020

RGB-Dome (ASCAP)
see Virgin Music, Inc.

Rhyme Syndicate (ASCAP)
2825 Dunbar Drive
Riverside, California 92503

Rilting Music Inc. (ASCAP)
see Fiddleback Music Publishing Co., Inc.

Rio Bravo (BMI)
see Major Bob Music

Rites of Passage (BMI)
see Warner-Elektra-Asylum Music Inc.

RMI (BMI)
Div. of R-Tek Corp. Inc.
8484 Wilshire Blvd, Ste. 650
Beverly Hills, California 90211

Rockin' R (ASCAP)
412 Oakleigh Hill
Nashville, Tennessee 37215

Rondor Music Inc. (ASCAP)
see Almo Music Corp.

Round Wound Sound (BMI)
see Bug Music

Rounder Music (ASCAP)
Address Unavailable

Roundhead (BMI)
1900 Avenue of the Stars
Los Angeles, California 90067

Rude News (BMI)
see Trycep Publishing Co.

Ruthless Attack Muzick (ASCAP)
3126 Locust Ridge Circle
Valencia, California 91354

Rutland Road (ASCAP)
see Almo Music Corp.

# S

St. Nicholas Music, Inc. (ASCAP)
1619 Broadway, 11th Fl.
New York, New York 10019

Saja Music Co. (BMI)
40 W. 57th St. Ste. 11510
New York, New York 10019

Salsongs
see BMG Music

Sawgrass Music (BMI)
1722 West End Avenue
Nashville, Tennessee 37203

Scarlet Moon Music (BMI)
P.O. Box 120555
Nashville, Tennessee 37212

Don Schlitz Music (ASCAP)
P.O. Box 120594
Nashville, Tennessee 37212

A. Schroeder International Ltd. (BMI)
200 W. 51st Street, Suite 706
New York, New York 10019

Screen Gems-EMI Music Inc. (BMI)
6255 Sunset Blvd., 12th Fl.
Hollywood, California 90028

Second Decade Music (BMI)
c/o TWM Management
641 Lexington Avenue
New York, New York 10022

Second Hand Songs (BMI)
see Super Songs Unlimited-Sealark

Seldak Music Corp. (ASCAP)
see Daksel Music Corp.

Seven Songs (BMI)
see Super Songs Unlimited-Sealark

Seventh Son Music Inc. (ASCAP)
c/o Glen Campbell Enterprises Ltd.
10351 Santa Monica Blvd,, Suite 300
Los Angeles, California 90025

Shakeji (ASCAP)
see MCA, Inc.

Shangmoto Songs (BMI)
921 Washington St.
Hoboken, New Jersey 07030

Shanice 4U (ASCAP)
see Gratitude Sky Music, Inc.

Sheddhouse Music (ASCAP)
27 Music Circle, E.
Nashville, Tennessee 37203

Shocklee (BMI)
John M. Gross, Esq.
51 E. 42nd St. Ste. 1601
New York, New York 10017

SHR (ASCAP)

Siete Leguas Music (ASCAP)
see Warner-Chappell Music

Silverline Music, Inc. (BMI)
329 Rockland Road
Hendersonville, Tennessee 37075

Siquomb Publishing Corp. (BMI)
c/o Segel & Goldman Inc.
9348 Santa Monica Blvd.
Beverly Hills, California 90210

Sir Spence (ASCAP)
1925 Century Park East, Ste. 1260
Los Angeles, California 90067

Skyfish Music (ASCAP)
Marquee International Inc.
P.O. Box 11400
Minneapolis, Minnesota 55411

Small Hope Music (BMI)
see Virgin Music, Inc.

SMICSMAC (ASCAP)
28 W. 69th St., #9A
New York, New York 10023

Snow Music
c/o Jess Morgan & Co., Inc.
6420 Wilshire Blvd., 19th Fl.
Los Angeles, California 90048

Solar (BMI)
see Kear Music

Sometimes You Win (ASCAP)
see Almo Music Corp.

Songs de Burgo
see Polygram Songs

Songs of Polygram (BMI)
see Polygram Music Publishing Inc.

Songwriters Ink (BMI)
see Forrest Hills Music Inc.

Sony Cross Keys Publishing Co. Inc.
c/o Donna Hilley
P.O. Box 1273
Nashville, Tennessee 37202

Sony Epic (BMI)
see Sony Songs

Sony Epic/Solar (BMI)
see Sony Songs

Sony Music Publishing (BMI)
see Sony Songs

Sony Songs (BMI)
P.O. Box 8500 (2320)
Philadelphia, Pennsylvania 19178

Sony Tree (ASCAP)
see Tree Publishing Co., Inc.

Sony Tunes (ASCAP)
c/o Tree Music International
8 Music Square West
Nashville, Tennessee 37202

Sounds of Lucille Inc. (BMI)
Music Administration Service Co.
c/o S A S, Inc.
1414 Avenue of the Americas
New York, New York 10019

South Heart
see BMG Music

Southern Gallery (ASCAP)
P.O. Box 150307
Nashville, Tennessee 37215

Spaced Hands Music (BMI)
see Beverly Glen Publishing

# List of Publishers

Sparrow: The Sparrow Corp. (BMI)
P.O. Box 2120
9255 Deering Ave.
Chatsworth, California 91311

Special Rider Music (ASCAP)
P.O. Box 860, Cooper Sta.
New York, New York 10276

Spectrum VII (ASCAP)
1635 Cahuenga Blvd., 6th Fl.
Hollywood, California 90028

Larry Spier, Inc. (ASCAP)
401 Fifth Avenue
New York, New York 10016

Spoondevil (BMI)
see Bug Music

Bruce Springsteen Publishing (ASCAP)
c/o Jon Landau Management, Inc.
Att: Barbara Carr
136 E. 57th Street, No. 1202
New York, New York 10021

Springtime Music Inc. (BMI)
c/o Andrew Feinman
424 Madison Avenue
New York, New York 10017

Srete (ASCAP)
see WB Music Corp.

Stage & Screen Music Inc. (BMI)
see Unichappell Music Inc.

Stage-Screen Music, Inc. (BMI)
c/o Careers Music, Inc.
Att: Mr. Billy Meshel
8370 Wilshire Blvd.
Beverly Hills, California 90211

Stansbury Music (BMI)
14613 Tiara St.
Van Nuys, California 91401

Starstruck Writers Group (ASCAP)
P.O. Box 121996
Nashville, Tennessee 37212

Billy Steinberg Music (ASCAP)
c/o Manatt, Phelps, Rothenberg &
Tunney
11355 W. Olympic Blvd.
Los Angeles, California 90064

Ray Stevens Music (BMI)
1707 Grand Avenue
Nashville, Tennessee 37212

Mike Stoller Music (ASCAP)
784 Park Avenue
New York, New York 10021

Stone City Music (ASCAP)
c/o Gross, Shuman, Brizdle
Laub, Gilfillan P.C.
2600 Main Place Tower
Buffalo, New York 14202

Stranger Music Inc. (BMI)
c/o Machat & Kronfeld
1501 Broadway, 30th Fl.
New York, New York 10036

Stratium Music Inc. (ASCAP)
c/o Meibach & Epstein
680 Fifth Avenue, Suite 500
New York, New York 10019

Street Knowledge (BMI)
see Unichappell Music Inc.

Charles Strouse Music (ASCAP)
see Big Three Music Corp.

Tom Sturges (ASCAP)
see Chrysalis Music Corp.

Sun Face Music Inc. (ASCAP)
152-18 Union Turnpike, Ste. 12R
Flushing, New York 11367

Sunstorm (ASCAP)
see WB Music Corp.

Super Songs Unlimited-Sealark (BMI)
200 W. 51st Street, Suite 706
New York, New York 10019

Al B. Sure International (ASCAP)
P.O. Box 8075
Englewood, New Jersey 07631

Keith Sweat (ASCAP)
Address Unavailable

Sweet n' Sour (ASCAP)
see Virgin Music, Inc.

Swizzle Stick (BMI)
see WB Music Corp.

# T

T-Boy
Address Unavailable

Taco Tunes Inc. (ASCAP)
c/o Overland Productions
1775 Broadway
New York, New York 10019

Take 2 (BMI)
3944 West Montrose
Chicago, Illinois 60618

Paul Taylor (BMI)

Taylor Rhodes Music (ASCAP)
210 Lauderdale Road
Nashville, Tennessee 37205

TCF (ASCAP)
see WB Music Corp.

Ted-On Music (BMI)
Gladwyne Postal
P.O. Box 376
Gladwyne, Pennsylvania 19035

Ten Ways To Sundown (ASCAP)
see Zomba House

Testatyme (ASCAP)
see Almo Music Corp.

Texas Wedge (ASCAP)
11 Music Square East
Nashville, Tennessee 37203

Theory Music (BMI)
see Screen Gems-EMI Music Inc.

Thousand Mile Inc. (BMI)
see Bug Music

Threesome Music
1801 Avenue of the Stars, Suite 911
Los Angeles, California 90067

Thriller Miller Music (ASCAP)
9034 Sunset Blvd., Suite 250
Los Angeles, California 90069

tHUNDERSPIEL (BMI)
see Bug Music

Tiger God (BMI)
see WB Music Corp.

Tillis (BMI)
see MCA Music

TJT (ASCAP)
see Warner-Chappell Music

Tol Muziek

Tony! Toni! Tone! (ASCAP)
see PRI Music

Tranquility Base Songs (ASCAP)
c/o Tom Shannon
5101 Whitesett Avenue
Studio City, California 91607

Tree Publishing Co., Inc. (BMI)
P.O. Box 1273
Nashville, Tennessee 37203

Tres Hermanas (ASCAP)
see Famous Music Corp.

Tri Ryche (BMI)
see Screen Gems-EMI Music Inc.

Trio Music Co., Inc. (BMI)
1619 Broadway
New York, New York 10019

Triple Star (BMI)
1875 Century Park E.
Los Angeles, California 90067

Trycep Publishing Co. (BMI)
c/o John P. Kellog, Esq.
33 Public Square, No. 810
Cleveland, Ohio 44113

Tuareg Music (ASCAP)
P.O. Box 903
Magnolia, Alaska 71753

Two Knight Publishing Co. (BMI)
c/o Copyright Service Bureau Ltd.
221 W. 57th Street
New York, New York 10019

Two Sioux (BMI)
Enter Prizin Mgmt.
c/o Al Scaife
4950 Wilshire Blvd.
Ste. 4000
Los Angeles, California 90010

Two-Sons Music (ASCAP)

# List of Publishers

Two Tuff-Enuff Publishing (BMI)
6042 Bellingham Drive
Castro Valley, California 94552

Tyreach (ASCAP)
see Almo Music Corp.

## U

Umbrella Day Music (BMI)
see Island Music

Unbelievable (BMI)
see Jessie Joe

Uncle Ronnie's Music Co., Inc. (ASCAP)
1775 Broadway
New York, New York 10019

Unichappell Music Inc. (BMI)
810 Seventh Avenue, 32nd Fl.
New York, New York 10019

Unicity Music, Inc. (ASCAP)
c/o MCA Music
445 Park Avenue
New York, New York 10022

Utilitarian Music (England)
Address Unavailable

U2 (ASCAP)
see Chappell & Co., Inc.

## V

Velvet Apple Music (BMI)
Three International
8 Music Square, W.
Nashville, Tennessee 37212

Vernal (BMI)
see EMI-Blackwood Music Inc.

Vesta Seven (ASCAP)
see Almo Music Corp.

Virgin Music, Inc. (ASCAP)
Att: Ron Shoup
43 Perry Street
New York, New York 10014

Virgin Songs (BMI)
see Virgin Music, Inc.

Vision of Love Songs Inc. (BMI)
Padell, Nadell, Fine, Weinberger
1775 Broadway
7th Fl.
New York City, New York 10019

## W

Waifersongs Ltd. (ASCAP)
c/o Michael C. Lesser, Esq.
225 Broadway, Suite 1915
New York, New York 10007

Walden Music, Inc. (ASCAP)
Att: Bonnie Blumenthal
75 Rockefeller Plaza
New York, New York 10019

Walker Avenue (ASCAP)
348 Carroll Park West
Long Bench, California 90814

Wally Songs (ASCAP)

Walter Afanasieff (ASCAP)
see Warner-Chappell Music

Warner-Chappell Music (ASCAP)
c/o Cathy Nolan
9000 Sunset Blvd.
Penthouse
Los Angeles, California 90069

Warner-Elektra-Asylum Music Inc. (BMI)
1815 Division Street
Nashville, Tennessee 37203

Warner-Tamerlane Publishing Corp. (BMI)
c/o Warner Brothers, Inc.
9000 Sunset Blvd.
Penthouse
Los Angeles, California 90069

Watercolor Music (ASCAP)
see Warner-Chappell Music

Wax Museum (BMI)
2438 East Cactus Road
Phoenix, Arizona 85032

WB Music Corp. (ASCAP)
c/o Warner Brothers, Inc.
Att: Leslie E. Bider
9000 Sunset Blvd., Penthouse
Los Angeles, California 90069

WE (BMI)
  Address Unavailable

Webo Girl (ASCAP)
  see Warner-Chappell Music

Wee B Music (ASCAP)
  Route 2, Box 466-B
  Ash Street
  Central City, Kentucky 42330

Welbeck Music Corp. (ASCAP)
  Total Video Music
  c/o ATV Music Group
  6255 Sunset Blvd., Suite 723
  Hollywood, California 90028

Welk Music Group
  1299 Ocean Avenue, Suite 800
  Santa Monica, California 90401

Willesden Music, Inc. (BMI)
  c/o Zomba House
  1348 Lexington Avenue
  New York, New York 10028

Willow Girl (BMI)
  20010 Calvert St.
  Woodland Hills, California 91367

Wilphill (ASCAP)
  see EMI-April Music Inc.

Wind and Sand Music (ASCAP)
  P.O. Box 324
  Bearsville, New York 12409

Windswept Pacific (ASCAP)
  4450 Lakeside Dr., Ste. 200
  Burbank, California 91505

Wing & Wheel (BMI)
  see Irving Music Inc.

Wocka Wocka (ASCAP)

Wonderland Music Co., Inc. (BMI)
  c/o Vic Guder
  350 S. Buena Vista Street
  Burbank, California 91521

Wordiks (ASCAP)
  see PRI Music

World Wide Music Co., Ltd.
  R.R. 2, Box 466-B
  Ash Street
  Central City, Kentucky 42330

Wrightchild (BMI)
  see EMI-Blackwood Music Inc.

# Y

Yellow Elephant
  see Sony Tunes

# Z

Zachary Creek (BMI)
  see Almo Music Corp.

Zappo Music (ASCAP)
  Att: Bruce R. Hornsby
  16815 Hartland Street
  Van Nuys, California 91406

Zen Cruisers Music (ASCAP)
  Hanson, Jacobson & Teller
  335 N. Maple Drive, #270
  Beverly Hills, California 90210

Zevon Music Inc. (BMI)
  c/o Jess Morgan & Co., Inc.
  6420 Wilshire Blvd., 19th Fl.
  Los Angeles, California 90048

Zodboy (ASCAP)
  13428 Maxella Avenue, Apt. 292
  Marina Del Rey, California 90292

Zodroq (ASCAP)
  13428 Maxella Avenue, Apt. 292
  Marina Del Rey, California 90292

Zomba Enterprises, Inc. (BMI)
  c/o Zomba House
  1348 Lexington Avenue
  New York, New York 10128

Zomba House (ASCAP)
  137-139 W. 25th St, 8th Floor
  New York, New York 10001

Zoo II Music (ASCAP)
  4205 Hillsboro Road
  Nashville, Tennessee 37215

Zuri (BMI)
  RZO Inc.
  9200 Sunset Blvd.

# List of Publishers

No. PH2
Los Angeles, California 90069

ISBN 0-8103-7485-4

90000